Man's ~~Best~~ Worst ~~Friend~~ Enemy

"From A Nightmare of Pain to a Life of Purpose"

Reggie Stoddard

Man's Worst Enemy

634 NE Main St. #1263
Simpsonville, SC 29681

Text Copyright © 2019 by Reggie Stoddard

All rights reserved. No part of this book may be reproduced, scanned, or distributed in any printed or electronic form or by any means without prior written consent of the publisher, except for brief quotes used in reviews.

Please do not participate in or encourage piracy of copyrighted materials in violation of the author's rights. Purchase only authorized editions.

Library of Congress Control Number-
2019936839
ISBN 978-0-998-0269-4-7

Printed in the United States

"Do not love the world or the things in the world. If anyone loves the world, the love of the Father is not in him. For all that is in the world—the lust of the flesh, the lust of the eyes, and the pride of life—is not of the Father but is of the world."

I John 2:15-16

NKJV

Contents

Foreword		5
Reviews		7
Introduction		8
Chapter 1	Knowing Your Foundation	13
Chapter 2	Understanding Purpose	21
Chapter 3	Blank Check	39
Chapter 4	The Power of Desire	55
Chapter 5	Beware of the Counterfeit	68
Chapter 6	Deal With the Roots	76
Chapter 7	Don't Ignore Warning Signs	85
Chapter 8	Embrace Your Suffering	92
Chapter 9	God's Word Will Keep You	102
Chapter 10	Pursue, Overtake and Recover All	110
Chapter 11	That "Best" Life	114
Chapter 12	Deal With Your Beast	119

Foreword

Ever so often, I come across a book that is essential for my collection. One that is so classic, I refuse to lend. I'm confident that this represents that type of book. This reading aides as a guide that instructs both men and women in their studies.

Reggie Stoddard is a warrior who understands how to relate to the hearts of men. I've had the privilege to know Reggie for more than ten years. Our initial introduction occurred when we were colleagues at Southern Wesleyan University. Reggie enriches all of our lives through his leadership, commitment to excellence, and devotion to serve. He's a man of his word whose actions are of the highest integrity. It has been with great honor to witness his faithfulness and unconditional love as a husband and father.

Personally, I am excited about this book because it relates to both genders. It unveils the significance of manhood, fatherhood, brotherhood, husband, and son. The vast majority of men wear a multitude of hats in life. It's a requirement that Christ remain at the forefront of our daily walk.

Man's Worst Enemy conveys topics to include purpose, potential, and even gives insight on the uncontrollable appetite men possess that can ultimately lead to destruction when you do not take dominion and authority. *Man's Worst Enemy* is designed to assist men in recognizing the pitfalls of sin. As men, we need continuous restoration. We're challenged with not expressing our pain.

Throughout the earth, men are crying inside for help, salvation, and long for the day they can feel safe to no longer internalize their fears. I pray that this book will minister to your spirit and that you experience a breakthrough of freedom. I decree and declare that your heart will be mended with answers to questions you have not yet been afforded the opportunity to ask.

Just as a soldier at war, we too must know where the mines are on the battlefield so that we're vigilant to not end up in terror. With that being said, men if you are longing to commune with God on a deeper level, produce meaningful lives, challenge yourselves to new heights, fulfill your purpose, and be the persons you were born to be, this is a must-read. I'll leave you with one of my favorite quotes. "He that reads will lead and he that leads must read." My prayer is that God will ingrain within you the desire to do both, read and lead!

~ Pastor Hasker Hudgens, Jr.

Reviews

An amazing book that bears all and tells all. With the spirit of lust that is so prevalent in our society today, here we have a pastor and an author willing to share his personal defeats and his victories. Praise God for this book, a must-read for all who have battled with the spirit of lust.

-Pastor Donnie O'Shields

This book is going to be one that is going to take you on a ride emotionally, spiritually, and cognitively. This book and its author are one in the same. They both are able to move you with testimonies that will touch your humanity while pulling you close to God. Read with understanding while the author shares moments of his life that just may change yours. At the end of this experience, you will have questions, but prayerfully more answers.

-Dr. Karras C. Cohen, Sr.

Introduction

This book was written for the enlightenment of a very common area in the lives of men and women where darkness has prevailed and because of shame and lack of knowledge of God's Word, we often fail to overcome. This project is greater than 20 years in the making! God's plan was to make sure that the author found deliverance, healing and freedom before publishing for anyone else. My experiences in life led me to a subterranean, below the surface study of God's Word. As a result, I came to the understanding that mankind, in general, has fallen to many things hindering us in a plethora of ways. However, if you truly look at the common denominator of this fall, you will find that mankind can't seem to get a grip on overcoming lust and addiction, the #1 enemy. Yet, we often mistake it as a friend. Ultimately, this leads to failure and lack of contribution to society. There is one thing that I have come to know over the years concerning men (although it affects all, I can only speak directly of men); most of us deal with our external issues, the things that others are aware of and see. But we treat our lustful nature as if it is our friend; we feed it, like a baby we nurture it, we protect it from exposure, and we continue becoming intimate with it. This is why at the end of the day we are deceived by it!

As a result, God has placed this book in my heart. You would think that the wisdom and knowledge of God would bring us to a place where lust or any other form of evil cannot overcome us. However, time after time, we continue to fall for that same trick that we have always fallen for over the years, since the beginning of time. We must realize that there are no new enemies that we now face that our forefathers didn't face. According to Solomon, there is nothing new under the sun (Eccl. 1:9). Furthermore, Paul tells us that the temptation we are dealing with is common to man (I Corinthians 10:13). That means we are not dealing with a new devil or a new form of evil. This is the same joker that enticed Adam and Eve. He is the same deceiver that called Abel and had his brother kill him. This is the same fallen one who has caused God's people to do such unspeakable evils currently being exposed in the church today! The same joker that caused havoc in every patriarch we read about. The same one that Christ defeated! Well, if this is true, why do we keep falling to the same tactics of an ancient enemy, of whom I must remind you, is already defeated? In the famous words of my former pastor, "that lion doesn't even have any teeth!" He is just perceived as a threat but he (the devil) has no power over God's people! It seems that we would have learned by now his devices and equipped ourselves with the anti-lust weapons of warfare. But daily, in myself and other men and women, I see different. This led me to a study of this area in my life, how God delivered me and others eventually, inspiring me to write this book in which I know God will use to minister to men and women of like nature, dealing with the same issues, bringing a God-driven impact to our lives. Although Solomon said there's nothing new under the sun, there is one thing that God says is new daily; that is His mercy (Lam 3:23)! No amount of experience, education, knowledge, inventions, wisdom, nor is there any other thing capable of bringing us out of bondage, but the **grace and mercy of God**. This is our only hope! It is because of God's mercies that we are not consumed! This text contains many discoveries and failures of mine and others. But most of all, it is an attempt to show God's view and plan for man's life according to the Word in spite of those failures. The intent is not to expose us but rather bring light into an area especially we as men like to keep in the dark for fear of falling to it ourselves. Because we have kept it in the dark, failing to expose it, we are now seeing men and women of God being exposed daily. As we sit by in awe, this should be no surprise! God will not continue to allow His church to idly sit while this thing wreaks havoc on the innocent! Jesus mentioned in John 3:19 that men loved darkness rather than light because their deeds were evil. Men, we have to expose the enemy to the Light of God's Word in order to live to our potential. This journey is not based on opinion but spiritual truth. Men love darkness! Why? Because we don't want to be exposed. It is not a myth but a reality. It has affected our families, destroyed our marriages, crippled our children, corrupted our occupations, and the list goes on. It has invaded our pulpits and church leadership. It has caused men and women of God to go astray and eventually perish, seeing the corruptness of our spiritual leaders. Devout men and women of God are divorcing, fornicating, and committing adultery while the church that was once encouraged by them watch in awe and the world sees no hope!

    I know what God called me to do. But before I came to this place in my destiny, there were some things I had to do. The very first step was acknowledging that there was an issue. I refused to continue protecting my secret life. I chose to expose the devil rather than wait on God to expose me! I chose to tell the world how it affected my life in order to show like people that there is TRUE deliverance and ultimately freedom. I AM FREE, PRAISE THE LORD I'M FREE! The devil is a liar! You can find deliverance and freedom in Christ no matter where you are or what you've done. The only problem is the thing that hinders us is mankind's # 1 enemy, LUST or what I call *Lacking Understanding in Sensual Trauma* – my personal commentary to unrestrained desire. Yet we hide it and protect this dark portion of our lives as if it is our best friend. Expose it before you are exposed! Call it what you must, but according to 1 John 2:16, everything *in the world* fits in to one of the three following categories: lust of the flesh, lust of the eyes, or the pride of life. It has caused me pure hell! No one wants to own up to it knowing it is our #1 enemy, yet we treat it as if it is our best friend. This reminds me of the myth that dog is man's best friend. That is a lie. I love animals but I will not place them on the level of a friend. It's just not biblical! Most men that are falling or have fallen to it have been blinded to the affect it has on their lives. They think this is some kind of trade or good gene left behind by their forefathers as if it were their friend. Ungodly desire doesn't love anyone. It is not at all your friend! It has come to steal, kill and destroy you! What does James 4:1 say?

"Where do wars and fights come from among you? Do they not come from the desires for pleasure that war in your members?" (NKJV)

Disagreements, wars, fights, and falling outs come from desire and lusting of ungodliness. Talking to men, it is minimized as just a small portion of their issues. But what they don't realize is that the enemy has seized them and minimized their view on the situation. In many cases as I wondered why, I found that many of these men love darkness! Until you call it out, it will remain inside of you and I warn you in case you did not know; to a real anointing, it stinks! As for me, I come against this spirit in the name of Jesus, the name at which *every knee* shall bow (even lust and sensuality), and every tongue shall confess that He is Christ the Lord!

Before I begin I want to thank God for his infinite love for my life. It is one thing to be loved but an entirely different level to have someone love your life. Paul puts it this way;

"That Christ may dwell in your hearts through faith; that ye, being rooted and grounded in love, may be able to comprehend with all the saints what is the width, and the length, and depth, and height; And to know the love of Christ which passes knowledge, that ye might be filled with all the fullness of God."
Ephesians 3:17-19 (NKJV)

Paul is telling us that the love of Christ goes much further than the eye can see, it is wider, longer, deeper and higher than the mind can comprehend, and passes all knowledge. This is much more than the love we know. Jesus cares for our life and purpose, not just us! For this we owe Him a lifetime of gratitude.

Next, I would also like to thank my wife, Leonnie, (AKA Lady Lee, my Boo, my Bae, etc.), the lady that has stuck it out with me throughout my battles while dealing with her own assignment and life changing battles. It hasn't always been easy nor has it been all promising, but we stayed the course. In the midst of it all, she was there knowing that God ordained her to be the helpmate in my life, for life. I could not begin to discuss some of the things she had to endure to stick by my side. I realize most would have packed up and been on their way. But she refused to choose the alternatives reminding me that those things worth having in life are the ones we'll struggle the most for. In 2019, 24 years and counting, we are more in love now than ever. It is a whole different dimensional type of love. A love that speaks without saying a word! A love that can only be experienced through Christ. All I can say is that it is a love you have to experience. Then there are our spiritual mentors (they don't like the word parents, lol), a true man and woman of valor sent to give us direction at the right time in our lives. I would like to thank Pastors Donnie and Dana O'Shields for sending a Word from God, fresh manna, in the time of desperation, oasis, crossroads and need for direction. I was tired, weak, and worn, but God, in the midst of hopelessness sent a man of God that had some stability in his life. Just when I felt like Elijah, "Lord I am alone; all the prophets are gone…" God sent him and his family to get us through this crossroad saying, "There is more in you!" He encouraged me when no other could as his help mate, Pastor Dana, loved my wife as her own daughter. I thank God for their model lives and their sharing with us as parents share with their children while dealing with life-changing ministry battles of their own. Thanks and may God bless and keep you, Robert Grant and Dr. Sonia Cunningham Leverette, for walking us through our initial authorship process. I can't call everyone's name, but God knows your name and thank you for your prayers and thoughts. Whether you meant them for good or evil, it was all part of my destiny.

Chapter 1
Knowing Your Foundation

It seems appropriate when building a house that we start with the foundation. It took many years for me to understand what was really meant by this metaphor pertaining to life. I had the basics but of the technical and spiritual depth I had no clue. Paul says,

"According to the grace of God which was given to me, as a wise master builder I have laid the foundation, and another builds on it. But let each one take heed how he builds on it. For no other foundation can a man lay than that which is laid, which is Jesus Christ."
I Corinthians 3:10-11 (NKJV)

Paul teaches us that as kingdom people, we all have been given a foundation that we are to build on. We have to stand for something! How can we stand and you don't know what you are standing for? You have heard the old saying, "If you don't stand for something, you will fall for anything." Kingdom is more than going to church and following rituals week after week. I watched the leaders in the church as I grew and it really disgusted me and curved my appetite for serving in the church. I witnessed men with no foundation doing any and everything, unaware of Who and Whose they were. They were looking marvelous in the suits, cars and houses but their spirit was a mess! Today is a new day and it is time out for playing church games. Know your foundation. What you stand for is much deeper than you and your family. There are generations depending on you and your actions. What is a man? He is the very image and likeness of God. From what I understand, when God is in the midst, the atmosphere must change. We are thermostats and not thermometers!

    Let's look a little deeper at foundations. What is the first part of a house that is built? If you know anything about building, you know that before a house or building is erected, earth is removed in the place the house will stand. Then there is some digging so that footers or pillars can be poured. This is so the foundation runs deeply into the ground and is not just surface deep. We cannot just grab a foundation and throw it down and start to build upon it. We must labor and look deep into what is true. Listen to how Jesus contrasts the man who built his foundation the correct way with the one who did not build wisely;

"Whoever comes to Me, and hears My sayings and does them, I will show you whom he is like: He is like a man building a house, who dug deep and laid the foundation on the rock. And when the flood arose, the stream beat vehemently against that house, and could not shake it, for it was founded on the rock. But he who heard and did nothing is like a man who built a house on the earth without a foundation, against which the stream beat vehemently; and immediately it fell. And the ruin of that house was great." Luke 6:47-49

    A foundation is actually more important than the house itself. A foundation will keep you grounded and faithful when the wind blows and the storms of life rage. I know men get tired of being tossed and driven by the wind. A foundation will keep you from infidelity when your spouse is not who you need or desire her to be. Men, we have to dig deep and allow the Word of God to penetrate our souls. The pastor cannot keep you in the midnight hour. He cannot keep your sanity when you feel like you're losing your mind. Only God can keep you when you need to be kept! Very seldom do I see men "sold out" for Jesus. Even in leadership, men are not rooted and grounded in the Word. We as leaders promote based on what we see and not what God says. This is the very reason men fall daily because they are not filled with God's Word and His Holy Spirit. The man who was sustained by the storms in Jesus' illustration "dug deep," indicating that he took some time and worked on what he would build upon. He planned his building and went down before he went up. You want promotion, exaltation, and honor? God says the way to go up is to go down… humble yourself before the mighty hand of God and He will do the exalting… This is something that we teach at Epicenter413. It is the foundation of our ministry. We learned that a tree actually grows down before it grows up! There is activity beneath the soil that we cannot see. These are the late night hours spent in prayer, reading and meditating on God's Word. All this takes place before we begin the building of our outward lives. Too often we push and promote based on contribution, looks, etc. Just because a man tithes or holds a position of authority in the marketplace does not count him worthy of leadership in God's house!

    I remember the first house that I built at the age of

27. After a bitter divorce, life got tough dealing with the battles fueled by my past. It was at this time in my life that I sought the God that I had been playing with for some time. It was time out for religion; I needed the presence of God. I needed an encounter. As a result, I repented and turned to Christ. Battered by life-changing issues, insecurity, hurt, pain, rejection and purposelessness (mostly fueled by self-infliction), I decided to get serious about His Word and attempt to walk the walk. See I am the kind of guy who is looking for something solid to believe in. I can't claim something and show a contrary action. In other words, I have a hard time being a hypocrite. Yes, I have been one in times past but it's not my character because it is too much work. During this time God really challenged my heart to the point that I was in a state of shock. Picking up the pieces of a broken life, divorce, and children out of wedlock and so on, I tried moving on.

Though heavy laden with issues, I was blessed to have an opportunity to have my house built. This was a long, tedious process that was frustrating to say the least. I had trouble out of the builder on several occasions. Needless to say, I did not do my homework before finding one. Of all the things that I remember, there was one incident that I will never forget. It was the winter months when the foundation was being poured. Temperatures reached well below freezing several nights in a row. One morning as I was riding by checking on the progress, I saw water gushing from beneath the cement slab, the foundation. I learned that the pipe underneath the slab had burst due to freezing the night before. I spoke to the builders and they assured me that this was a common and insignificant repair, posing no threat to the integrity of the home. Little did I know I was in for a treat! Nonetheless, the house was completed with much disagreement between the builder and me.

Finally, I moved in the spring of 1999 with much joy. After a year passed, I began to experience many issues that characterized my faith walk. It started with the increasing presence of critters, such as spiders and crickets. I noticed that my room and closet were like an ice box in the winter months. I remember looking for a pair of shoes in my closet one morning. While on my hands and knees crawling, I saw light in the darkest corner of the closet. This is when I discovered the nightmare. The frame of my house had separated from the foundation! In haste, I ran to the outside of my closet and found that the concrete slab had sank about six inches into the ground and the house was leaning. Immediately, I contacted the builder.

What I learned is that when the water line burst during the building process, all of the dirt was washed from underneath the house. As a result, the concrete slab sank several inches on one side of the house. During the course of the year, the walls cracked, doors did not close and the list goes on. But remember the builder told me this was normal for new houses and that I would have to "wait until the house settled." Really? See this is the problem with this life. We think we are okay with shortcuts because we cannot see the immediate results. It took more than a year for this error in building to manifest. While I had no clue, all of the issues that I thought were normal were actually a result of a failed foundation. This really spoke to me about my life and it provoked me to turn to God.

As much as I thought I had it together, I could hear the Spirit of the Lord telling me that my issues flowed from a heart that had a cracked and broken foundation. It was at this point in my life that I realized how important a good foundation is. I was a new preacher and a servant in the church, but God had to shift some things in my life. It was at this point God had to teach me that I don't compare or judge my life by other men, but by the Word of God. Yes, I'm talking to those who feel they are okay because they don't do what some do or compare themselves to other men as their measuring sticks. We have to work out our own salvation! This was the turning point of my life. What you have may look good, but if it isn't built on the proper foundation it will fall.

Are you rooted and grounded in the Word of God? When God allows the storms of death, loss, disappointment, failure, etc. to blow in your life, will you stand? Are you standing? Or, have you heard what God requires and failed to make the necessary adjustments? Keep reading…

Chapter 2
Understanding Purpose

In order to fully understand the importance of our escape from our #1 enemy or our assigned giant, we must first realize who we are and the very purpose of our being. Who we are has everything to do with what we deal with, which makes it essential to figure out! Men have failed to take into consideration what's at stake when it comes to the subject of why we were created. **We must understand purpose! Webster refers to purpose as, "an intended or desired result, a determination."** We are not just someone being born out of error without purpose. Listen, God knows our names! And He has not forgotten about us! We are the very seed God has placed to bear fruit for the nations.

"He saved us and called us with a holy calling, not according to our works but according to His own purpose and grace, which was given us in Christ Jesus before the world began." II Tim 1:9

If we truly get the revelation of that Word, my God it will unlock some doors! It basically says, "What we are going through really has nothing to do with us!" Let that simmer… We must understand that God laid out His plan for our lives before the world began. That alone should get us excited. It's not because of who we are but Whose we are. We are the very source of our family's providence. We are a representation of who God is. We are somebody's hero and source of direction. We have a God-given purpose and design that our Father has entrusted us with. Men, get this in your heads: It is not about you! It's about your children, grandchildren, and the generations beyond.

You say you are born in sin, have no father or don't know him, it seems no one cares whether you live or die, you wasted away your life on drugs, are incarcerated, diseased, poor? Well, guess what? Other powerful men of God, including myself, who are now His servants with the difference of knowing who we are and a glimpse of why we are here, shared these same experiences.

I can't ever forget the many times I've seen (and see) men walking through life without a purpose. Most of them wake up daily with a belly full of regret. Do you know what that feels like? I cannot help but notice that in most cases, these men have children out there whose lives they are not involved in; thus, if no one teaches them who they are, they too will follow the same steps. We are currently raising what is called the "Fatherless Generation." Who will teach them? Who will show them the way? Who will help them avoid the same life that we escaped? The world?

Yes, I have failed in this area too! What really bothers me is that many of these men that I witness in the world living riotously are actually in better shape than they realize. They have two or three children, (some more) wrapped up in the system of child support, eventually leading them to just give up all effort of living a quality life. These men have no sense of purpose and as a result have no passion. ***Purpose ignites passion***! I say again,

"***Purpose ignites passion!***" This reality put fear in me because I knew in one day I could be in the same boat if I didn't do something different with my situation. There I was having children by several different women! I realize that there are worse cases out there, but let's face it, that's enough! I can never forget the fear that was in me of the years to come. I always asked, "Where will I be in ten years, five years, or even next year?"

Seeing other men was like seeing someone suffer abundantly for a crime while you, having committed the exact same crime with more power to it, did not have to suffer as they did. It will almost make you say that isn't fair because I deserve worse, but instead I became grateful, realizing that in a twinkling of an eye I could be homeless and without hope. That's when I learned that favor isn't fair. What is the difference between them and me? I found grace! In that grace, I found my purpose. I know who I am and when you know who you are you have overcome! When you know God and have a relationship with Jesus, you'll learn that, "Where sin abounded, grace did much more abound," according to Romans 5:20. What that means is this, just because we messed up does not mean that God has thrown us away. Paul tells us that not many noble are called… In fact, because we messed up, He has bestowed His grace upon us to cover our mess! His grace is sufficient for all our needs. His love never fails, never gives up, never runs out on us!

While I initially thought God would take it all away, He just gave me grace to overcome. Oh we will suffer the consequence, but MY GOD, the grace He gives will blow our minds and have us asking, "God, who am I that You are mindful of me?" Therefore, my heart goes out to those who are caught up in the system and feel as if there is no hope.

Man or woman, there is NOTHING too hard for God! One of my biggest mistakes was not sharing with anyone my heart issues (as if no one knew). My family made comments, but no one dared ask me how I was dealing with it because they didn't know how to help me. And don't mention the church! They just talked about me behind the scene and I felt so isolated in the church, especially in ministry. It was like I walked in a comedy club and the joke was on me. People saw the hand of God on my life, but they could not see past my past. They looked at me when they should have been looking "in" me for the hope of His glory. Those who knew me felt sorry for me, condemned me, or didn't know what to think. But the fact of the matter is that I needed help! I needed Jesus, and the church could not give that to me. They could not minister to me! To this day, no one has told me or asked me how I was dealing with my broken past or asked me if I needed help. But I knew there was something greater than that.

When I got saved, something happened on the inside of me and to this day it still drives me like a hungry lion. It's so deep that it could not be cured with all the food in this world. Now, I realize that God is my source. While I was looking to man for acceptance, I was being rejected. It is a terrible feeling to be sick and no one sincerely asks how you are doing. This is why to this day when I get the opportunity, I look a man right in his eye and ask him how he's doing. It took me a while to learn that this burning, yearning, unquenchable desire was purpose. And I now understand God allowed me to deal with this alone to understand the need to help others.

I once read Ecclesiastes 4:11 and Solomon said, "He has put eternity in men's hearts…" Now I understand what it is that won't let me go. It's purpose! I couldn't die if I tried to. When I got a hold of God's love for my life, dying wasn't a choice anymore. No matter what I do, God is always whispering in my ear, "Reggie, there's more in you." When I feel like it's the end of my rope and want to quit, I hear the voice of eternity whispering, "Eternity." There's more in us men! There is more in you women! More than you'll ever know. Just when I thought I had nothing to offer, I heard God say, "There is more in you, son." But God, how is there more? I am done, have nothing to offer, made too many mistakes, let too many folks down, spent all my resources… At my weakest point, when I had nothing to offer, God said, "Now I can use you."

So, I hate to rain on your parade, but no devil in hell, no obstacle, or no hater is going to allow you to achieve your destiny without a fight! In fact, God allows this in order to strengthen us in our sight of the vision He has prepared for us. David said, "My affliction was good for me. It taught me your ways." I had to learn to count it all joy.

It is impossible that no offenses should come…!
Luke 17:1(NKJV)

I don't know anyone walking in purpose, who is

achieving, has achieved a goal or has made it without offenses. Have you read the Word lately concerning Moses, Abraham, Isaac, Jacob, or even Jesus? They all had to face offenses on the way to their destiny. Jesus says in Matt 19:26, *"But with God all things are possible"* (NKJV) and I thought that I could go through life believing that one day I would arrive at a place where the offenses would stop or be easier to handle. However, I have learned what it meant when Jesus spoke of the wise and faithful servants when He said, *"To whom much is given, much is required,"* that the greater the anointing, the greater the offenses. The greater the assignment, the bigger the giant. Just understand this one thing, if you choose the road with *no* obstacles, in the end it costs *just as much* as it would have if you had chosen the road with obstacles.

Proverbs 13:15 says, *"...the way of the unfaithful is hard."* (NKJV) What Solomon tells us is that even the way of the wicked is hard. What is the way of the wicked? The easy way out that does not involve Jesus! So why not suffer for discipline instead of consequence? There will be suffering! That thing, that lust, those evil desires are there to destroy you and keep you from reaching that goal, or prize, that Paul was referring to in Philippians 3:14. They are there to frustrate your purpose. As Zerubbabel and the leaders tried to rebuild the temple during captivity, the Bible says,

"...then the people of the land weakened the hands of the people of Judah, and troubled them in building, ...and hired counselors against them, to frustrate their

purpose...." Ezra 4:4-5 (NKJV)

Men we must realize that we are the temple of God! As we walk in our God-given purpose, we are rebuilding the temple and the enemy has dispatched counselors in order to frustrate our purpose. They come in all shapes, sizes and colors and yes, some of them seem to be really good lovers... It's the temple of God they are after. There is nothing you are dealing with that has not already been conquered! Someone has already defeated that giant and if God did it for them, He will do it for you... This thing is not about us! We have to press toward our goal, that higher calling on our lives. It will not come without our efforts daily. What good is a land that costs us nothing to obtain? The children of Israel had to be puzzled about God's idea of the Promised Land. Why would He give us land that is already occupied?

Well, even the kingdom of God suffers violence and the violent take it by force. We have to fight for what belongs to us or the enemy will take it. In fact, it was prepared for us! All we have to do is to go in and possess it! We are so busy trying to build our own kingdom when God has already built it for us. The battle is the Lord's. All we have to do is stand still on the promise. Those giants of lust and evil desires have held us back from the promise too long. They are eating OUR grapes, OUR bananas, and that fruit God has promised us. What will we do? Settle for less? Will we allow the enemy to fool us into false hope, satisfying us for a season then leaving us in famine?

Well, I advise you to get up from that rut, that ungodly relationship, that unprofitable means of provision, and walk into your destiny, sore into your dreams. Your purpose must be your priority. This battle is not about someone trying to stop you, nor is it personal, but the enemy knows what the outcome is going to be if you reach your destiny. Do you get it? This thing is bigger than you! It's bigger than the "American Dream." Don't let the enemy fool you into thinking your situation is not that bad. I dare you to try coming out and you will begin to see the intensity of your situation. I never knew my situation was so intense until I met God and tried to come out. I had to learn that anything worth having is worth a fight. Hebrews 6:12 (NKJV) reminds us that we "Be not slothful, but followers of them who through *faith and patience inherit the promises*." Through faith we keep walking regardless of what we see around us or the things we suffer; we walk in patience because we know when to stand still and see God bring us through it. We cannot sit by idle (sluggish/lazy) waiting on God to bless and deliver us.

Again, I say, this thing is bigger than we are. I get so tired of the enemy taking us out because we choose to sit and allow him to destroy our families and our children's families. Someone has to break the chain of curses passed on to us. Divorce, children out of wedlock, fatherless homes, rape, and molestation have not only invaded our homes but have invaded our churches. The pulpit is infested with lust, as well as the choir, and the list goes on. Satan has boldly entered our sanctuary and set up his throne while we, the watchmen, sit as spectators. And what do we do? Nothing! Why? Because we ourselves are not free and remain afraid to approach the area in which we continue to struggle. Come out from among these transgressions and be different. I would rather have a church that pleases God than one that is full of carnality! Answer this question: If you, yeah you who are reading this, do not pray for your loved ones and intercede for their future, then who will it be? Do you care?

What is your purpose? What is your biggest dream that you are afraid to go after for fear of failure or exposure because of your past or present situation. There were dreams and visions that God gave me, but I was afraid to pursue due to my condition. I knew that God would not bless me in my mess. As a result, I sat and was disarmed of my zeal to go after what was mine. Don't get it twisted. Regardless of what you see, if a man is living a carnal, sinful life, God is not in it and whatever he appears to be prospering at will get tested. I realized that if I put my mind and energy in it, I could still do some things, but with no anointing it was useless because it would not last. Do you know how dangerous a man is without God? Think back to Genesis 9:11. Nimrod, the son of Cush, the son of Ham, the son of Noah (Genesis 10:6-8), a mighty hunter before the Lord was the builder of Babel and other great cities. In Chapter 11, with Nimrod as their leader, the people came together and said,

"Let us build a city and a tower whose top will reach the heavens." And they started to build so God looked upon this and said, *"The people are one and nothing will be restrained from them that they imagine to do!"* Gen 11:4 (NKJV)

The point is this, the will and power that God gave us is for us to do *His* will. But often, out of rebellion, we want to get back what we lost in Adam, our own way and make our own name great, as we see in this passage. This is why we see the wicked seemingly prevailing. They have taken their God-given talent, as Nimrod did, and used it to try to establish their own way. As you see, God will only allow so much so why not carry out His will, His way.

Therefore, knowing that God requires our all, we will either try to do it without Him and seem to progress for some time but utterly fail, or not do anything for fear of facing our #1 enemy and coming clean so God can have every part of our life, even the parts we ourselves are afraid to see. David said in *Psalms 51:6,*

"You desire truth in the inward parts…"
(NKJV)

Oh, how hard it is for men to bring our all to God. Can you imagine what you can do *with* God on your side, seeing what He said about Nimrod and those that rebelled against Him as far as how they appeared to be prospering? In fact, you don't have to look at Nimrod. As stated earlier, God has placed eternity in you and eternity says to you, "Son, if you let go and let God, your possibilities are endless. There is more in you!" There comes a point in our lives that we have to break down and just be real with God and in some cases, the people in our circle. I went so far in ministry but I kept finding myself back at the same place, cycles: not coming to truth in my inward parts! I had done all I could do in and of myself.

Man's Worst Enemy

I once preached a sermon entitled, "I Have Gone As Far As I Can Go Without Faith!" I could go no further. Not even preaching the gospel would get me through this! My charisma can't fix this. No amount of money could help me. So that promise, vision, and those dreams that were in me would not manifest because I needed to deal with that shame of lust, desires and self-sufficiency deep inside and some of the things it drove me to do I had to face. God could not birth His promise in me without total sell-out to Him. I knew I was unstoppable with God but *only* if I surrendered all! The dreams and visions in my heart were so unbelievable that I was afraid to half-heartedly enter into them.

Unfortunately, this same condition I see in other men who are not totally sold out but they are trying to walk in God's divine purpose. You have seen them; they get so far in that ministry that seems so anointed and prosperous and at a twinkling of an eye they are in the paper or have pulled out of ministry because of something they have done or someone has discovered. Then, you see them confessing the truth (in some cases). What keeps you from that God-given dream or purpose? Are you completely sold out? Let me help you. If you are not sold out to God you will never reach your potential. Man, there is more in you!

I remember seeing myself in visions walking in the promise of God, like Adam in the garden, in the purpose and love of God. So, I ask myself, why can't I do this when I see this? What is it that holds me back? Why do I continue to go in cycles and end up right back in the same place? On the right track for a season, then discouraged again. This is the same wandering that Israel did for 40 years because they could not totally trust and depend on God. It was fear of failing and my lack of trust in God. I tell you the truth, I have loved God a long time and I knew that after all I had been through He was the only one that could change my life and correct my course. But I found even in loving Him I was still holding back. And because of this He could not entrust me with His blessings.

Men, it's time to let go and allow God to begin a healing and deliverance in your lives. It is time to get back up again! Winners never quit and quitters never win. You are purposed and anointed to suffer as Jesus did until you reach your destiny. One thing that really struck my heart and still this day rings in my head is what I heard the man of God (Bishop Getties Jackson) once say. His exact words were, *"You must care for your purpose and your destiny more than your feelings."* He says this is a major part of what kept him clean and pure. We all know that once the thrill is gone, we are right back at ground zero, empty! Knowing this was one thing but to hear him say it with an intense anointing drove it in my heart like a stake. I had to ask myself, "What do I love more - feeling or destiny?" This is a reality check. Emotions will have you tossed about like a ship on an angry sea. As men, we cannot get wrapped in emotion. The time we waste pondering on our heart's desires of life is immeasurable. Oh, how much time I wasted! When it comes down to making choices, there are only two, life and death. There is no in between where it will not affect the rest of our lives and generations to follow. This is why Joshua said (Joshua 24:15) that we have to make a choice in whom we are going to serve. If we look at our choices in this manner, maybe we can make better choices. After all, each choice is a matter of good and evil, life and death according to Moses (Deut 30:15). I encourage you to choose life and purpose…

Like Nature

There is a story that I want to share. One morning, the Spirit of God woke me around 5 AM. In a vision the Spirit said to me, "I want to show you something concerning purpose. I need you to see how important it is that you obtain it, embrace it, and walk in it all the days of your life! When I got up, my mind began to play a strange narrative. I pictured a rabbit eating a carrot. As Rabbit was eating Carrot, everything was normal, like nature. But something happened and it totally interrupted all of life's natural processes. The Spirit said to me, "I want to show you what happens to man when he decides to abort the intended purpose for his life." So, as I was watching Rabbit consume Carrot, a natural scene (this is why it is called nature), time stopped! I mean literally, time stopped! Clocks stopped ticking! And the strangest feeling came over me and all that I could encompass. Everything was weird! But the Spirit seemed to not have an interest on anything except me watching Rabbit and Carrot. As I stood in awe and under a wealth of other emotions, He said to me, "Focus on Rabbit and Carrot." It wasn't what He said but what I felt Him saying in my spirit without a word. Though in amazement, I gathered my emotions and turned back to the scene. This is when I saw the most unnatural, live, animated act I had ever seen in

Man's Worst Enemy

my life. And it was not on TV, it was real! Rabbit dropped Carrot from his mouth. Yes, he immediately stopped eating and dropped Carrot on the ground. Then I saw him stand up like a human and he looked around like the matrix as if something was terribly wrong (remember time stopped).

I was in awe! I was flabbergasted! Words cannot express the thoughts that were in my head because I could not put it in words. However, I was kind of amused at the same time. It was something like the feeling I get when I am on a roller coaster or airplane; I take a break from the fear and try to enjoy the ride while leaning on God in faith that my life is in His hands. So, he (Rabbit) drops Carrot and the scene begins to get more and more unnatural. Carrot stands up (I didn't know carrots had feet). And it was like he was about to say, "Hey, why did you drop me?" But he didn't. He said to Rabbit, "Rabbit." Rabbit, looking around, says, "Yea, you see that?" Carrot asks, "What just happened?" Both were in a daze and looked in all directions as if someone or something was stalking them. And me, not knowing how to feel, whether I should laugh or cry, was in a deadlock stare with what was going on with them.

Now as if this scene couldn't get any more out of the box, something else happened that totally got my undivided attention. When I saw this next turn of events, my focus was more in tune not with the awkwardness. I began to ask, "What is really going on?" It was like I no longer was a spectator, but I actually entered the scene and became like Rabbit and Carrot, "Do you guys see this?" But I was still in tune with the Spirit as if I were having an out of body experience. He (The Spirit) didn't say a word but I could feel Him say, "Now I have your attention." Then I saw a wolf. I had seen him sneaking up on Rabbit just before all this got weird as if he was going to eat him alive. But when time stopped I became so focused on Rabbit and Carrot that I just totally tuned him out. So, Wolf stopped his pursuit of Rabbit, being only a few feet away. He then stood up on his back legs, and Rabbit said to him, "Something's not right!" At this point I was supposed to pass out but it was strange; I was calm and at peace. It was like my mind could not handle this so my spirit took over. Here we have a carrot talking to a rabbit when the rabbit is supposed to be eating a carrot. Then the rabbit turns and starts to hold a conversation with his upper echelon in the food chain who was about to rip him a new one! You get it? A wolf and a rabbit carrying on a conversation like two humans! I know, I can't believe I am writing this. I am not your average Looney Toonist... As these three carried on a conversation, I began to see everything in nature become unnatural. Even the grass, the ants, the birds and every living organism began to stop all natural activity and turn animated, but so real. At this point I needed to ask someone what is going on. I turned to the Spirit and I asked, "What is going on?" "I thought you would never ask," He said. "You see, time has stopped. And I wanted to show you that this is how purpose works" "Purpose," I asked? "What does purpose have to do with what I just saw?" The Spirit says, "Let me explain. See, to you, time is natural. Rabbits eating carrots is natural. A wolf in the process of eating a rabbit is natural. Then, you look at nature and you see something strange like animals and living organisms start to malfunction because time stood still and you say this is totally out of order..." "But it is, isn't it?" I said. Then Spirit says to me, "Is it? Well I look at you in that same manner." "What do you mean?" "Well, when you're not walking in purpose, as you were created, all of heaven does the same. They are in awe because it's so unnatural to them that the Father created you before the foundation of the world and you, like time, seem to forget to continue on your course. Now that's unnatural!"

Then I immediately came to! I found myself at my computer having written the entire scene down. Point taken! What we have seen in nature every day we call it natural when it's nothing but what God has already purposed. The rabbit is doing exactly what it was created to do. So was the carrot, the wolf, and all the other created things. But when time, which is purposed by God, decided to halt, EVERYTHING went bizarre. None of these creatures were acting out until time acted differently or out of purpose. Likewise, when man is not in purpose, nothing else works natural like it should. Wives begin to act out; children cut up. Finances don't know how to line up. Dreams can't reach their designed destiny. All because you, man, are not in purpose! Like the creatures in the scene, everyone and everything pertaining to man and assigned to him stops its intended purpose and begins to act out of element!

Get in purpose man! And the "Whole universe will conspire to make things work in your favor." We were created to worship God. Ephesians 1:3-9 (NKJV) says

"Blessed be the God and Father of our Lord Jesus Christ, Who has blessed us with every spiritual blessing in the heavenly places in Christ. Just as He chose us in Him before the foundation of the world, that we should be holy and without blame before Him in love, having predestined us to adoption as sons by Jesus Christ to Himself according to the good pleasure of His will, to the praise of the glory of His grace, by which He made us accepted in the Beloved. In Him we have redemption through His blood, the forgiveness of sin, according to the riches of His grace which He made to abound towards us in all wisdom and prudence, having made known to us the mystery of His will, according to His good pleasure which He purposed in Himself, that the dispensation of the fullness of the times He might gather together in one all things in Christ, both

which are in heaven and which are on earth – in Him!"

Chapter 3
Blank Check

This is a very unique chapter. I learned some important lessons through experience, study and observing others. We all have an appetite, but if we don't seek understanding we will be abused by it. In II Samuel 12, Nathan the prophet confronts David. We all know the story. David, when he should have been tending to his purpose as a king, planning and preparing for the people of the kingdom, (*hint: II Sam 2:11 "at the time when kings go out to battle"*), stays back at the mansion when others are following the vision. Meanwhile, back at the mansion enjoying too much downtime, David decides to head to the rooftop to get a glimpse of his domain.

Again, I cannot stress enough that when we are not walking in purpose, we will self-destruct. Where there is no purpose, abuse is evident. I don't care how great the intentions, there are some desires and appetites in us that will quickly pervert and lead us astray when the focus becomes anything less than God. Jeremiah says in 17:9, "The heart is deceitful and desperately wicked. Who can know it?" Meanwhile, back at the ranch… David sees the forbidden fruit of his servant Uriah, his wife Bathsheba, and he has to have her. You all know the story and if not, please read it.

Now if you have been in church any amount of time you know how the story goes… He desires the fruit of his servant and pursues her. After his desire is conceived, there is a turn of unexpected events leading to adultery, lying, murder and the list goes on. Nathan the prophet approaches David. In their conversation, Nathan tells a parable of a rich man and a poor man. There was a poor man who had nothing but his family and a lamb that he regarded as a child of his own. This lamb grew with his family and even ate from the same table as his child. When a traveler arrived in town, he came to fellowship with the rich man. In preparing for the traveler, the rich man did not consider his own substance. Now that alone is a preaching/teaching word! He did not consider all he had to give but desired to take from others who were less fortunate. The prophet continued explaining that he (the rich man) went to the poor man and took his only possession (the lamb in which he regarded as his own child), and slaughtered it for his guests.

When David hears this, the Bible states that "His anger is greatly kindled." Imagine that the king bursts into anger concerning this harsh, inconsiderate, rich man. I need you to feel this! Then the king immediately lays down the law, delivering a harsh sentence regarding the rich man's deeds saying, "The man shall surely die!" Little did King David know that the joke was on him! He is the rich man the prophet is speaking of in the parable. My, what a turn of events. Finally, Nathan drops the bomb and reveals to him, "King David my friend, you are that man!" Imagine that! (I'm sure that teaches us a lesson; before we point fingers, we should check ourselves and maybe we will avoid the embarrassment of always considering the other person being the issue). After Nathan reveals to David he is the one who has sinned or he is the rich man who he is so angry with, Nathan says,

Man's Worst Enemy

"Thus sayeth the Lord, I anointed you king over Israel and I delivered you from the hand of Saul…I gave you your master's house and your master's wives into your keeping, gave you the house of Israel and Judah… <u>if that had been too little I would have given you much more.</u>" II Sam 12:7-8

    As I studied the life of King David, one of the major lessons I learned about him is that he had a big appetite. He is not the only one but he is definitely one that God has given us a panoramic view of his life. Here is the issue that God revealed to me about King David; instead of asking and seeking <u>God</u> for more, though he loved God, he chose to fulfill himself through what he saw in Bathsheba. I would like to think that we are in many ways like the king wherein we have a desire and feel like it's too much *or* God is not concerned about that part of our lives! Listen, God loves every part of you! It's not a secret that God gave David what he needed and then some! He was a blessed man. Anytime we search for more without God, we begin to lust for it ("For all that is in the world… is not of the Father…"). It is no longer a desire but a wickedness. Don't allow your weakness to become your wickedness! It's alright for men to have a big appetite. Again I say, it's alright for men (and women) to have a big appetite. There is no sin in that. Just read the whole chapter as we apply wisdom to it. The problem begins when we don't understand our appetite and its origin.

    Now what I am about to say may defy some

religious beliefs. Here it is; please understand that our appetite was created by God. Yes, God created us to be fruitful and multiply, fill the earth and subdue it and have dominion. How can we do this without an appetite? How can we be created in the image of El Elyon (God Most High) or El Shadday (God Almighty) or El Olam (The Everlasting God) without having an appetite? HOWEVER, it becomes a snare when *we try to fulfill what God has created outside of His will.* You hear that? The appetite you have was created by God. How can I say God created this in me? In Psalms 81:10-13, God says, "Open your mouth wide and I will fill it." Again I say, "Open your mouth WIDE and I will fill it!" One more time for the Holy Spirit: "Open your mouth WIDE and I will fill it!" This scene reminds me of birds before their mother with their mouths wide open. They expect a filling that will satisfy their hunger. In that same sense, we are to approach God with our mouths wide open so we may be filled of and by Him. Go back and read Psalms 81 and you will see that God wants to provide every need, every desire but only after we have come to Him! It is time out for preaching physical prosperity without soul prosperity. Now had David, in his time of wantonness, opened his mouth praising God, (because in every situation praise is what we do), God would have filled that void that he tried to fill with Bathsheba. The bigger your appetite, the bigger your praise ought to be. We have to cease from wantonness. Put a praise on it. But take it a step further; put a praise on it just because He is able. That will catch up with you on a later date. Are you feeling a lack? Are you feeling a need for a filling? "Open your mouth wide" so God can pour into you. Read the whole chapter about how God warned Israel not to have any other god before Him and how these gods would destroy them. He desires for us to come to Him to be filled. Stop complaining about your spouse. Stop complaining about your job. You have a big appetite? Let God take care of it. Only those who are hungry and thirsty will be filled. There is NO lack in the kingdom. David wasn't experiencing lack. He was experiencing void, a deep calling from God.

Listen, I have learned that physical pleasure will surfeit (make us full), and never satisfy, but spiritual pleasures will satisfy and never surfeit (Isaiah 55:2). That 16th (last) verse of Psalms 81 says, "He would have fed them (Israel) also with the finest wheat; And with honey from rock I would have satisfied you." Won't He do it? This is what I love about God and the reason I keep that praise and worship on deck. He has a way of doing things that keep us in suspense. He said, "The finest wheat..." You don't have to apologize about having the finer things in life. God desires you to have them. Just make sure you acquire it through Him and His process. It's not just okay but necessary to come to Him with a "wide open mouth." This doesn't mean begging God for stuff! We are God-seekers. That means we seek God (Matthew 6:33) and stuff chases us. We don't chase stuff. Gentiles, non-believers, worldly folk chase stuff. He also says, "...and satisfy them with honey from the rock." Honey from the rock? God says to me in this passage, "Son if you set your eyes on Me with a mouth that glorifies Me, even in your need and desire, I will fill you with a new thing from a place you have never even thought of!"

In Psalms 103:5, He also says, "Who satisfies your mouth with good things, so that your youth is renewed like the eagles." The problem with that filling you are getting on your own, the one David got, is that it is leading to your death. I know you may feel you are losing in this world and that you are insignificant. But Paul says in 2 Corinthians 4:16, "Do not lose heart. Though our outward man is perishing, our inward man is being renewed day by day." This is what the psalmist was saying. When you trust God to fill you, your "Strength is being renewed like the eagle," just as Paul says, "Your inner man is being renewed day by day." Trust me on this one: You will not die, I promise. You are looking for love in all the wrong places, and catch this; you are looking for it in all the familiar places. We who belong to Christ don't do what the world does. You see they are getting caught up (if they are called… ooops!!!) Do you have a call on your life? Are you the chosen? Then, God will not allow you to go on without getting caught. Yes, getting caught is what's best for you. Let that simmer a minute; Selah. I would rather get caught in my foolishness and repent than to continue on and wind up in eternal damnation. Let's move on and take a look at these next few scriptures:

*"I will praise thee; for I am **fearfully [and] wonderfully** made: marvelous [are] thy works; **and** [that] my soul knoweth right well."* Psalm 139:14 (KJV)

"Before I formed thee in the belly I knew thee; and before thou camest forth out of the womb I sanctified thee, [and] I ordained thee a prophet unto the nations." (Jer 1:5 KJV)

David says, "I am fearfully and wonderfully made…" Jeremiah says, "Before I formed you in the womb I knew and approved of (sanctified) you." We ought to shout right there. God says He formed you and when He finished, He approved of it. If He created it, approved of it, will He not finish and fulfill it? You have been praying that God removes those desires and God is saying, "I know you. I created you. Now let Me fill you! I want you to have the finer things in life. But I want to be the One who supplies. I want to show you a new thing that will renew your strength like pulling honey from the Rock! But you are so focused on "it" without Me when I just want you to bring it to Me with a WIDE OPEN MOUTH." Jesus says in Matthew 5:6,

"Blessed are they who hunger and thirst after righteousness, for they shall be filled." Matt 5:6 (KJV)

Jesus assures us that if we have a hunger for the righteousness of God, we will be filled. What does that mean to you? According to the Amplified Bible, He says, "…for they shall be completely satisfied" God has ministered to me in that I realized if my focus is on our relationship, then He would fill me in all aspects. In Matt 6:33 he says also,

"Seek first the kingdom of God and all these things will be added." Matt 5:6

So please understand, God created you and it was

good. Let me reiterate, God created you and it was good! What happens is this: when we are feeling empty and lonely we seek to be filled by the physical and we fail to allow God to fill the void that HE created. In fact, He created it that He might have you come and "Open wide." I understand the void that we as men and women are faced with daily. Many of us are searching for something more in our homes, so we blame our wives. We are searching for more in our churches, so we blame our pastors. We are searching for more on our jobs, so we blame our bosses. But it's all an attempt to fulfill a God created void. When we begin to desire things, sex, money, companionship, etc. we should seek God's kingdom. Just open wide.

As my former pastor says, "Go make love to your gift!" You're trying to live two, three or four lives, just go to HIM! I had to learn a valuable lesson; first of all my wife cannot completely fill the lack that I have. Secondly, no other person(s) nor possession can fill my lack. God keeps us in a state of longing for Him so that we never get to a place where we are satisfied in a person. Yes, when we are desiring something, it is a void that God created and the enemy is trying to duplicate it through lust. Please get this in your spirit. People, including your spouses, will never satisfy what God has created in you. This is always a prelude to adultery, fornication and molestation to name a few when we make our spouses God. So what happens is all too familiar day in and day out. This is what David was dealing with. When he should have been making love to his gift (out to battle being that he was a man of war), he was on the roof top looking around, with idle time, similar to the way we surf the internet, flip stations, and look through phone contacts. He took advantage of the powerful anointing on his life. One thing I learned about this anointing on my life, not only will it attract attention but it also magnifies and intensifies my desires. Therefore, I have to stay in God's face and keep my mouth WIDE OPEN! I have a big appetite but I found out that it's okay. I stopped asking God to take it away and began asking Him to fill me up. We fail to understand what we are searching for; thus, we substitute the spirit of God for the spirit of lust. *We must understand that <u>God has given us the appetite and only He can fill it</u>! Anything less than that only keeps us in want.*

"You're addicted to thrills? What an empty life! The pursuit of pleasure is never satisfied."
Proverb 21:17 (MSG)

    Once again, this is a teachable moment, lust can never be satisfied. You can only fuel it. The more you feed it, the more it wants. Again, the more you feed your physical, the more it will desire. It fills (surfeits) but never satisfies. Lust cannot satisfy you, unlike the Word of God, which satisfies but never fills to a point where we want no more (surfeit)! In other words, you can never get enough of it. Lust only grows in desire increasing in intensity after each feeding. It's like a growing lion; you see it as a baby all cuddly, gentle and harmless. But know this; that lion is a wild beast that will grow and revert to its original purpose to become king over its territory. You are raising the beast to destroy you!
    I once heard an interesting analogy by Harold

Man's Worst Enemy

Thomas, one of the leaders of Epicenter413. He told the story of a young lady negotiating with a snake because she was warm and the snake was cold. The negotiation was that she would allow the snake the warmth of her bosom inside her jacket if he agreed not to bite her. After convincing the snake not to bite her, she picked him up, took him in her coat and provided warmth. But the snake bit her 100 times! As she was dying, the woman said to the snake, "I thought we agreed that if I helped you that you would not bite me?" But the snake said to her, "Lady, you knew I were a snake when you picked me up." The moral of the story is this: Stop picking up snakes. Paul says in Romans 8 that the carnal mind is enmity (hostile) against God. It cannot be subject to Him. There is no negotiating, dialoging or debating. This is war! There is no stopping point. Sin (fleshy desires fulfilled) will take you farther than you want to go, keep you longer than you want to stay, and cost you more than you want to pay! Ungodly, sinful, lustful relationships WILL bite you at some point. You are making a deal with the devil.

Did you not hear what the prophet spoke to David in II Samuel 12? *"I gave you all of those things and if that were too little I would have given you much more!* God is saying to us, "My grace is sufficient." You have enough because I know what you need and desire. *If it takes more I will give it!* Can't you see that God wrote David a blank check? He didn't say I would have given you another wife. He says, "such and such…" To me, that means we don't know what we want. But He does. Therefore, open wide and let Him fill it. Let your worship fill out the check! OMG! Your worship ought to reflect your appetite! I'm talking true worship, not just praise. This is why David finally realizes in Psalms 23, "The Lord is my Shepherd (provider), I shall not want!" Men and women must get the revelation that when the Lord is our Shepherd, there is no want (lack). Try filling a gas tank with diesel fuel; it will not run!!! This explains to me why so many times we run from house to house, relationship to relationship and still we find that although it may be enough for that moment, after the fact we are all the more empty. We are filling without satisfaction. Isaiah displays reality in the following passage;

"Ho! Everyone who thirsts, come to the waters; and you who have no money, come, buy and eat. Yes, come; buy wine and milk without money or price. 2) Why do you spend money for what is not bread and wages for what does not satisfy? Listen to me and eat what is good and let your soul delight in abundance." Isaiah 55:1-2 (NKJ)

In other words, that thing which you have substituted for abundance and filling is only wasting your goods for something that could never fulfill you. The analogy is this: *Being **fat** doesn't mean we are **full or satisfied**! It just means we have a big appetite and we are eating a lot of the wrong stuff!* Many of us want to follow God but our selfish desire keeps us from total commitment. We cannot commit to God until we discipline our lives and surrender our will and desires to Him. I am a witness that God will give you the desires of you heart according to His Word, and you don't even have to tell Him what you want. Again, I have received some of the deepest desires in my life and not opened my mouth to God or anyone else! My twins are one example. I never even mentioned to my wife or God that I had a deep desire to have twins. In fact, with all the fornication and mistakes I had already made, how dare I ask for twins? I'd created too much mess already and I didn't deserve it. But God! When I began to delight myself in the Lord as the scripture states, my did He blow my mind without even one word! We don't have a clue of what God has for us! Just worship Him; delight in Him. Of course, that comes when we learn to operate in the mind of Christ. Yes, this includes things right here on earth.

I am not super spiritual and I have desired to see and have some things in this life that God promised right here on earth. We just have to be ready for them and not allow things to have us. Once I learned this principle and allowed God to be Lord over my life, then I began to see some things manifest in my natural life. I also had to learn that when God says "no" it's for my own good. And the excitement and beauty in His "no" is that He has something *greater* for me that will make me rich and cause me no sorrow (*when you finish running around the room keep reading*). I get so tired of my fellow saints claiming God is in some type of blessing when they borrowed money or spent all their resources or robbed God with their tithes and offerings in the process of acquiring it. Yes, I said it; in many cases we rob God to buy a car, a home, a vacation and say, "Look at what God blessed me with!" Really? What Bible are you reading? The Bible says, "The blessing of the Lord makes one rich and adds no sorrow!" I'm sorry if it sounds harsh but I am angry with the devil and those of us who don't preach the truth. This is not a blab and grab, "throw a dolla and holla" type of anointing on my life. I don't want anything from you. I just want everyone to get this and know that this Word WILL work if you work it! This is the gospel of grace but is also the gospel of responsibility. I told Epicenter413 that we no longer have excuses to not live for God and to live our best life. The truth will make us free. God helps us stay on track and preach the unadulterated, infallible truth. Here is the key, if we truly desire to follow after Christ, Jesus says,

"...If anyone desires to come after Me, let him deny himself, and take up his cross daily, and follow me"
Luke 9:23

People of God, there is nothing wrong with wanting more! It is that pure God-given spirit of dominion within that says, "Enlarge my territory." You just have to realize that what you really want is more of God. Begin to ask God to fill you. Ask Him to fill every void in your life with His love. Men, there is more in you! Remind Him that He created you in His likeness and in His image. You think God has a small appetite? It is His responsibility to complete you but only those that "thirst and hunger" will be filled. Are you hungry for Him?

Challenge of Self Denial
Now here's the real challenge. It's one thing to be denied of something by someone other than you. But when Jesus says "You deny you, *then follow Me*, (Luke 9:23)" He challenged us. What He says is in order to come to me,

you have to prove to me that you are willing to put away some things by self-denial before I can truly help you. Trust me, Christ is not going to deny those things for us. And it is a vain prayer to ask God to humble us! Yes, it is vanity for us to ask God for humility. We are to humble ourselves just like we are to deny ourselves. There are some areas in our lives that God is saying we have to commit to changing. This is an attribute of His love, freedom to choose! It's not a bad thing. Once we make that commitment the Holy Spirit will help. There are some things we just cannot take with us into the kingdom! And we can only be helped when we really want help. Oh, we can initiate the change in others but at some point in the process there must be a willingness for them to help themselves. Think about this for a moment: It would be awesome if the things we wanted outside of God's will were all denied by Him. But reality is that we have to make a choice because He chose us. We as parents deny our children when they are too young to understand the difference. But as they come of age there must be a shift in responsibility of our children to take on their own decision making. If we want them to mature, we must allow them to make their own decisions. It took some time before I could understand what the forbidden fruit in the Garden of Eden represented. One way to look at it is that it was a form of freedom, freedom of choice. God does not make us love or choose Him. It's our choice, our freedom to love Him. But understand that freedom comes with boundaries. From the beginning of mankind, God has given us freedom but it came with boundaries. "Of every tree of the garden you may FREELY eat…" But He comes right back with the boundary: "but of the tree of knowledge of good and evil you shall not eat." Consider a river. It flows so freely but even a river has banks (boundaries) that restrict its flow. Why? Because if there were no banks (boundaries), it would become a swamp with stagnant water that stinks! This is why Joshua said choose this day whom you will serve. We have to make a decision. Life is nothing but a series of choices.

Where the Spirit of the Lord is there is liberty. Liberty is freedom to choose. But Paul reminds us that that freedom must not be used to our own advantage. We must leave our own desires and lusts behind and allow God to fill us with righteousness rather than filling ourselves with filthiness! Why is that so hard? Because of self, simply put. It's one thing when others deny us something we want or crave. But when we are held responsible for denying ourselves, we really get into a battle. Knowing this, we should always be careful not to put ourselves in a position that causes us to be tempted. We have to have a Joseph spirit and learn to run from situations that are conducive to our weaknesses. Stop trying to be a hero and run. Run Joseph, run! Again, Jesus says, "...deny yourself..." In essence, He says that no one else is responsible for you but you. And to deny self is to make a statement that Jesus is the one I trust to fulfill me in every aspect of my life, even my desires. Just know that the beginning is always hard. But always remember the purpose of God's grace and that it is sufficient as He gives you more and more strength in His grace to just say no. We no longer have an excuse. We are responsible for denying ourselves when it comes to lust and fulfilling evil desires. Can you do it alone? No! Jesus sent the Holy Spirit to help us in every aspect of our lives. Once we make the choice, He will aid in carrying it out. This is very important: the battle is in making the choice.

Once our minds are made up, then God will walk with us. In fact, He will do it for us. Our responsibility and fight is in the faith. The battle belongs to God so fight the good fight. In other words, just show up at the battle scene and God will do the fighting! Why do you think Jesus said He would send His Spirit once He was gone? It is so we can live a clean and Godly life. Remember the battle is not of flesh and blood but of powers and principalities (Ephesians 6). But we have to show up with our faith intact. The weapons of our warfare are not flesh and blood but spiritual. To fight a spiritual war, we need spiritual help. My prayer is that the people of God get freed and realize that physical filling is just a distraction that keeps us from our spiritual filling that fuels us for purpose. Learn that our appetites are a void that God has created so He can fill it. He wrote David a blank check ("I would have given you such and such…") and when we go to Him, He will do the same for us.

Chapter 4
The Power of Desire

This is a very important issue, that we understand exactly what lust is according to the Word of God. I would like to start with a scripture that God has opened my understanding to.

"For the love of money is the root of all kinds of evil for which some have strayed from the faith in their greediness and pierced themselves through with many sorrows."
I Timothy 6:10 (NKJV)

It seems farfetched but with God's help you will understand how this ties in to lust. As I was preaching one Sunday, God began to reveal something in this scripture to me. The thing that caught my attention from the beginning were the words "all kinds of evil." From the first time, I read the passage, I thought: *"Can all evil begin at the love of money?"* (Some versions say, "All *kinds* of evil."). Basically, according to KJV, the word <u>all</u> is used. Before we move forward let us read the previous verse in 1 Timothy 6:9;

"But those who desire to be rich fall into temptation and a snare, and into many foolish and harmful lusts which drown men into destruction and perdition." 1 Timothy 6:9 (NKJV)

Okay, let us start with money; we all know that money (in

the natural sense) has power in this world today. In essence, it rules. To move things in this world, you just about have to have money, again in the natural sense. Even Solomon says in the B clause of Ecclesiastes 10:19, "...money answers all things." But we need to clarify this before moving forward. Many have gotten this passage out of context (not reading the Bible in its entirety – line upon line, precept upon precept). If you read the entire passage of Ecclesiastes 10:19, you will get a better understanding. Money answers <u>*things*</u>, not the true necessities of life (*man shall not live by bread alone*). If you really look at this topic closely, you will realize that any kind of self-gain in this world relates to money, which simply states that money equals self-gain. Do you agree? If this statement is true, we can narrow it down to this: *"...the love of <u>self-gain</u> (money) is the root of all kinds of evil."* If we break it down, we realize that all kinds of evil is somehow linked to self-gain, something we have ungodly desire to obtain. The main reason it is so hard to worship is simply because it has nothing to do with us; it's all about Jesus! There is no such thing as "self" in worship. The reason most non-believers and even some unfaithful believers cannot grasp the entirety of Christ is due to the fact we cannot totally rely on and trust in Christ to fulfill us in *EVERY* area of our lives. Lust is a form of *self-gain* that becomes the root of all kinds of evil. In fact, money and things we possess with money open the door to evil temptations. This is partly the reason we need to seek the kingdom first so we may mature in our relationship with Him before we start receiving material blessing! I once heard a preacher say, "Hell is nothing more than selfishness on fire." Scary isn't it? You will find that typically any of us that end up out of God's will or in a backslidden stage, can somehow link our prelude to some type of selfishness. In a nutshell that's lust, our desire to please ourselves rather than trusting God to do it. There again *our concern or love for self (gain) is the root of all kinds of evil.* If Eve had trusted that God had her best interest in mind and not let the serpent entice her into believing He was holding back and keeping the "good stuff" from her, would she have listened to a serpent? No. She would have possibly replied, "My God shall supply all my needs and from me no good thing will be withheld, you foolish serpent!" Who would commit adultery on their spouse if they were not concerned about self? Who would turn their back on their brother, sister, friend or family if self-fulfillment weren't the root of it all? What other explanation can we give? Typically, the excuse in such cases tends to be, "Well, he/she wasn't there for me when I needed them," or "I wasn't getting fulfilled," or maybe "they were holding me back!" What happened to the vows, "Until death do us part?" What if God broke covenant when we go through? No! He keeps covenant having NOTHING to do with us! What happened to choice? Isn't life really just a series of choices? In any situation or circumstance we encounter in this life, we are faced with making a choice and at the end of the day we are responsible for that choice. What we cannot control is the consequence. This I found was one of my greatest awakenings in life; take responsibility for your choices because you have no control over the consequences! It will cause you to think twice, for one. And secondly, it will cause you to avoid wasting time in the "man up" process, suffering of the consequences and moving on. Remember what James says,

"What leads to strife (quarrels and fighting) among you? Do they not arise from your sensual desires that are ever warring in your bodily members? 2 – You are jealous and covet (what others have) and your desires go unfulfilled; so you become murderers (To hate is to murder as far as the heart is concerned), you burn with envy and anger and are not able to obtain so you fight and war…"
James 4:1-2a (Amplified)

    What you have is someone not getting what they *thought* they were due to receive or they see something else they think they want. James explains that our real issues are because of our own lust and desires. It's not our spouse's fault that we are not filled. It is not our employer's fault that we are not feeling appreciated or lacking what we deserve. What we are looking for is not in them. What we need cannot not be found in things… But "*money* answers all things…" So, we'd rather seek the money so we can answer the things we desire. Easy because it requires no relationship… Let that simmer a moment.

    To everyone that has ever even thought of walking out or giving up, I urge you to weigh out the cost and the consequences and give God the chance to fill that void in us the way He intended. After all, until we seek God's fulfillment, we'll always be in want. Most of the time, we will see that the enemy has actually turned those God-given desires against us so that we end up as self-seeking as he is. I have found myself in many counseling sessions with couples who are ready to quit, throw in the towel and forfeit what God has ordained only to learn that the common denominator to all these couples was a lack of fulfillment. I find myself telling couples that they are making their spouse their God by expecting them to fill a void that He has created for Him. God never intended marriage to decrease our time with Him. In fact, it requires more time and devotion to Him to make it as beautiful as He intended. Again, marriage is a mystery only found in Christ. I don't care how many friends you have, how close you and your spouse may be, if you don't have a relevant and fresh relationship with Christ you will be empty! Company does not equal fulfillment. You can be around a world of folks and still be lonely. It just means that you have a harder time being alone with Jesus. Don't aim to please yourself or expect anyone else to. God, your creator, purposed you for His glory and praise and is your source of fulfillment.

  I am a witness that God will give us the desires of our hearts if we focus on Him (Psalms 37:4). That spouse you feel you need to trade in for an upgrade, God will turn that relationship around and turn your hearts to one another, but the key is denying yourself. Those children you sometimes wish you had considered before having, or you feel were a mistake, God will cause you to fall in love with them like never before. When I began to seek God to help me with my overwhelming desires and my loneliness in spite of my companionships, He led my spirit to pray that my heart be turned to my wife and children and their hearts be turned toward me. There is joy at *your* table, there is peace at *your* table, there is fulfillment at *your* table and whatever you need is at *your* table, not at anyone elses! Stop looking for another table and set yours up the way God desires. Take that thing that the devil meant for evil and allow God to turn it around for His glory. I never thought I could love my wife the way that I do. But God, who is rich in mercy and grace, began to honor my marriage when I honored Him.

So many times, we see something that appears to look better than what we have. Or, it seems that it's just right for us. But I encourage you to ask David if the grass was greener on the other side. There is a blessing in the grinding! Keep working at it! You say, "Well, David went on and married Bathsheba and had Solomon," and so on. Did you read the whole truth and nothing but the whole truth? Did you read what God said to David concerning the hell he would endure for his sin? Did you read the entire story? Or do you look at some folks that have gone on from a broken marriage due to infidelity and think that God hasn't dealt with the sin? You better believe that God will have the final say. Yea, we can all repent and move on but God deals with sin on *EVERY* level and the consequences, like the struggles, are real! Did you ask them what it cost? Did you ask their children how the broken covenant affected them? I am not saying that there are no cases that are better off, just saying that there are probably more that can be fixed if people submitted to God and flee selfishness fueled by lust. I just believe that God can fix it!

I am also convinced that everything God created

has seasons: summer, fall, winter and spring. What we may be seeing in our spouse is someone at their very worst season that may need some encouragement. Instead of focusing on their issues, see if you have what it takes to brighten their life instead of allowing it to be a stepping stone for separation. I dare you to find the queen (or king for the woman) in your current situation! You might like it!

What we have to understand as people of God is that we have to go through ALL seasons in order to grow. We don't completely secure love at the marriage ceremony. It took years for my wife and me to test our love for one another. It took hard times, good times, sick times and a whole lot more for the love to grow and become what it is today. We cannot expect the season to be the same all the time. This goes both ways; if you are in a hard season right now, things have to get better; if you are in the best season right now, there will be hard times. Find the best in the person you are with instead of looking for it in someone else. Face the challenges so you can have a testimony in your dry season that will keep you focused on what God can do and has done. I consider the hand that I have dealt and been dealt to be a project that God is grading. I refuse to do anything less than my best as I long to hear Him say, "Well done, my good and faithful servant, well done. You took what was *impossible* for man and now have a testimony that it is possible for God." Lord have I grown! I became so tired of jumping ship, relationship hopping, always looking for the next best thing. Control those desires and find the jewel in your current situation *or* the next time you commit, commit for life! Without self-denial, this is virtually impossible.

Let's sum it all up to make sure we are on the same level. The dictionary definition of lust is) "1) *intense or unrestrained sexual craving, or* 2) *an overwhelming desire or craving.*" Basically, lust has as its focus pleasing oneself, and it often leads to godless actions to fulfill one's desires with no regard of the consequences. Lust is about possession, consumption and greed, regardless of the consequences or the havoc that follows. It's like someone who will go through any extreme to get money: fall out with best friends, lose respect, dignity, etc. It is that inner call to fill selfish desires and it is fueled by selfishness, but when the source is dried up it searches for the next source. You can easily recognize this feeling or desire by keeping this in mind, it has nothing to do with God. When you get what you want out of a relationship, are you ready to move on? Or do you always seek to give first? This will tell you whether or not it is self-seeking. Check your motive; it never lies. If you really want to test a relationship, take flesh out of it! Stop feeding the desire!

Now, knowing lust is a start. Nevertheless, some practical applications go along with knowing a thing according to God's Word. You can see we are the best at knowing something or someone. We go through an entire lifetime of relationships knowing people. How many of them do we understand? I was reading Proverbs 4:7 one morning and the Holy Spirit revealed this thing unto me; the wisdom that Solomon speaks of in this passage is Jesus (knowing Jesus is the principal thing). So He said, "Get it" which again is Jesus: But He goes on to say, "In all thy getting get understanding." Then it dawned on me that many people know Jesus and the basic principles that He teaches. However, do we really understand Him and His purpose? We are told here to seek to understand (the wisdom of Jesus) as well as we know Him. We all claim to know God but lack the understanding to live for Him. Have you ever known someone for a long period, and later in life found that they became a huge contributor to society or some great entrepreneur and you had no idea it was in them? I have. And I went through grade and middle schools with this person never taking the time to see the ambition in them. Likewise, have you known someone who later became a menace to society and you were totally blown out of the water? I guarantee, had you truly understood those people in the beginning you would have had some insight of their end (rule not exception).

    Sadly, this is the case with Jesus. Many of us know Him but don't truly understand Him and His purpose, or shall I say, the kingdom of God or His way of doing things. Ask the disciples when they expected Him to call down fire from heaven, rule with an iron rod (Luke 9:51-54)... In this same sense, we should seek to know and understand Him as well. Jesus warned that the thief only comes to steal, kill and destroy, but He (Christ) came to give life and give it abundantly (paraphrased). So, everything that is not of God means you evil. Don't only seek to know who the enemy is but understand him as well. When you understand a person, you know what they are trying to do and you know what it takes to defeat them. In most cases, they will not surprise you later in life.

    Now that you are obtaining wisdom, make sure you understand lust and its purpose. It is to destroy mankind.

Psalms 78:18-33 tells the story of the children of Israel and to what end their lust and desires led them. As you read, you see that they tempted God by asking Him for meat for their lust (verse 18). Basically, they wanted God to fulfill their pleasures for the *wrong reasons*. They didn't understand the struggle. While they were thinking God was denying them good, He was preparing their hearts to trust HIS provision and direction. James 4:3 says, "We ask of God that we may consume it for our pleasures (paraphrased)." While God was trying to teach them a valuable lesson (total dependence on Him), they were concerned about getting what they desired. And as I stated earlier, we fail to believe that God will sustain and keep us. In turn, we, for our own desire and pleasure, tempt Him. In verse 19 they asked, "Can God furnish meat in the wilderness?" This signified unbelief in His provisions and plans for them. And when God began to give these things, they were *still* not satisfied. As you can see, lust will eventually turn to your destruction.

    I am a living testimony that God will give you the desires of your heart; however, we must first give Him our hearts. Learn to trust God and trust in His provision knowing that He created you and He will sustain you! "No good thing will be withheld from those who walk uprightly (Psalms 84:11)." In fact, God wants to fulfill your desire. But we must understand that His desire is to purify us first. Initially, I did not understand Psalms 37:4 when David said, "Delight yourself in the Lord and He will give you the desires of your heart." We always get the second part, "He will give you…" but we must first delight in Him. I will try not to get too deep, but Lord knows I can because

God allowed me to experience this on another level! It started after my understanding what delight means… We as men especially, have a hard time with the delight part (women have no issues and that's why they know how to get blessed). The word David used in Psalms 37 for delight is the Hebrew word "**Anag**." This word means to be ***soft*** or ***pliable*** (easily bent, flexible) and figurative of the word "*effeminate,*" which means *having or showing characteristics that are typical of a woman or unmanly*! In fact, in most cases that we use this word, *effeminate*, it is used in a derogatory and disrespectful approach. But real men know who they are and are able to cameo in whatever character God desires in order to reach those in need!

    Now before I move on let's get a few things straight: one – there are no wimps in the kingdom of God, two – this is the attitude that we have towards God. Sometimes, it is necessary to lay aside the macho man and love our brother the way God loves us. Again, I say sometimes! I will become whatever I need to be in Christ to be accepted by Him because I know He desires to bless my soul inside out. So I say this, I have learned through this passage that I really did not know what my heart's desires were. Yes, I was clueless of what I wanted. Until I began to delight (become easily bent, flexible and effeminate) *in the Lord,* allowing Him to purify my heart.

    I had no clue the things I really desired. Except we truly worship God, we are clueless of what we desire of Him. I continued to face a relentless fact and reality; this desire thing is too powerful to ignore so I must seek God for the answer. This is why we must transform, be broken, flexible and effeminate in Him. Sometimes when we are hard core we only think of the needs and desires of a hard core man. Look at the warrior, blood shedding, general type of man David was. Yet he transformed in the site of God; he became effeminate in the presence of God. This caused me to go from always asking God for things in prayer to using my prayer time to open my mouth in adoration, praise, and worship, which resulted in seeing the manifestation of the things I desired without even asking. Wow, that will take some time to marinate. Don't take my meekness for weakness. If you don't know, you better ask *my* Goliath!

Please understand I am not making this stuff up. Again, I am a living testimony and those in my circle have experienced the same manifestations of God. God moved on my heart to do a series on prayer that lasted six weeks in 2018. It blessed my socks off along with others. Stop begging God for stuff in your prayer time and transform into a worshipper. Matthew 6 tells us that He knows what you need before you ask. Seek first His kingdom and righteousness and let Him do the adding in the right timing. Gentiles chase stuff; kingdom saints seek God. Stop chasing stuff and *seek* Him. When we learn to seek Him, stuff will begin to chase us.

Elder Larry Calhoun, one of the leaders at Epicenter 413, says, "We don't have to chase God because He is not running from us. We just need to seek Him!" Many of you are running but not going anywhere. Stop running, sit down and start to open your Bible and seek God. That's why David said in Psalms 23 after He made the Lord his Shepherd, "Goodness and mercy shall follow me ALL the days of my life!" He sought God and stuff chased him! I watched my family move from Pain to Purpose and have witnessed other families do the same mainly due to a shift in focus. I learned that I don't have to open my mouth with constant requests (there is a time for everything) because He knows what I need, desire and what's best for me. His Spirit lives within me and He knows the mind of God. Stop asking God for what you think you desire and delight yourself in Him. It is too powerful for you to handle. He will align your desire to Him and then reveal to you what your true desires are. If you don't have an intimate relationship with Christ, you really don't know what you desire! You don't know what you need. Are you trying to replace God with a thing? Meditate on that! Are you looking for Him? First, deny yourself...

Chapter 5
Beware of the Counterfeit

To counterfeit means to imitate something. Counterfeit products are made in the exact image of something valuable or important and are often unauthorized replicas of the real product. Counterfeit products are often produced with the intent to take advantage of the superior value of the imitated product and have the intention to deceive or defraud. With this in mind, it is important that we discuss some characteristics of our enemy. As we mature, this should be a concern knowing that the enemy is always using counterfeit (generally what we consider blessing) as a means of deceiving God's people.

Paul tells us in II Corinthians 2:11, "Lest satan should get an advantage of us; for we are not ignorant of his devices." It is evident in this context Paul was speaking on forgiveness. But this is true in many other facets. Paul says we are taken advantage of through ignorance of satan's many devices. With this being the case, we must look at the tactics he uses, signs of them and most of all be able to recognize him early so we may react before he takes root in our hearts. We have to realize, though, that we are God's children. We still have to be knowledgeable to watch and pray. Though God's children have wisdom, even the elect are being deceived. One of the leading downfalls of God's people is the absence of tactics or failure to operate in the spiritual warfare using the weapons we have been equipped with. Instead we fight with carnality (flesh) or throw in the towel. It is sad seeing my brothers and sisters in Christ that are not aware that they are being used or led by godlessness. We have been blinded by our desires. Tactics are actions or strategies carefully planned to achieve a specific end and are essential to reaching maturation in our walk with Christ. Do you realize that the enemy has plans for you too? What is your next strategy to overcome? Or do you just wake up in the morning hoping you make it through the next trial, temptation or attack? Unfortunately, many of us do not and will not reach maturity as it requires being led by the Spirit of God. Our weapons of warfare are not carnal!

Now the word device that Paul used in II Corinthians 2:11 is the Greek word Noema (no-ay-mah). It means a perception, purpose, the intellect, disposition, device, mind, thought. Paul is warning that we cannot be ignorant of the way the enemy thinks, his purpose, his disposition, his mind… We are so caught up in how it feels, we lose sight of his purpose. He came to kill us, to steal from us and destroy us period. This is how he is taking advantage of us; we are so caught up in what we see, feel, hear, taste and smell. Satan's mind is to mimic all that God does and is doing from the beginning of time. We are so quick to fall for the bamboozle. Let's wake up. Everything that glitters ain't gold (in the voice of my grandmother Catherine). This is why the spirit of discernment is so important, allowing us to avoid being taken advantage of. How do we recognize him? The Bible teaches us that we should know them by their fruit. In essence, godliness is motivated by love and it always puts Him first.

Man's Worst Enemy

Once I heard Bishop Getties L. Jackson, pastor of Kingdom Assembly Outreach Center, say, "Don't let him get his claws in you." Being at a low point in my life, satan was working overtime trying to take over my dreams, my vision, ministry, my life. This is when we are most vulnerable, especially when we are at the verge of breakthrough and ready to throw in the towel. But at the very same time, this is when God is most present in us. He that has begun a great work in you will perform it until the end... Yes, I was fighting for my life but I was fighting a losing battle until I decided that this was God's battle! All I had to do was stand on it. We cannot lose our sensitivity to God's spirit. We cannot allow our conscience to be seared. This is why maturation is so important. Once we lose that grip, it's a slow fade; there is hope but few find it. Like Esau, we become frustrated and trade the blessing of God for a morsel of bread. The morsel of bread is that ungodly relationship or that desire we continue to cater to when times get rough. It is those things we trade for our anointing. Esau soon learned the consequence of selling his birthright due to hunger pains.

We must learn to suffer; it is good for us. Although Esau tried to get out, all odds were against him; though we look for hope and repentance, they seem impossible to obtain. Why? Because we have ignored God's small, still call for so long that we just get to a place where we don't hear His voice any longer. It's there but the noise has drowned it out. People of God, this is a terrible place to be but there are so many church-going folk that are not hearing God and just as many that have not truly experienced salvation. If you are going to church and not hearing from God, you are in a critical situation! This is scary. We have to be honest and think about where we are in our walk. We could be right on the verge of a total loss, getting ready to walk off a cliff, walking directly into a lion's den. And face it, we will not turn out like Daniel either. Why? We refuse to walk in the footsteps of Daniel. Total surrender to God is what we need.

Looking back, this was a horrible thought. Satan had his claws in me. I was walking around like a dead man pretending to be alive. I had an Esau spirit and in church every Sunday and Wednesday. I was gifted but not anointed. For me to be here doing what I do is nothing short of a miracle. Fortunately and gracefully, the realization hit me; with God we can come back from anything. With God ALL things are possible. I was a repentance away from restoration. We have to swallow that pride and seek the Lord, even if it means that we need to get some help. It is God who gives us the victory through Jesus Christ. If we are not hearing from God regularly, we need to do the last thing that He told us to do.

Now let us embark on "counterfeit" a bit deeper. There are two forms of spirit (love & good / evil & lust). And they are unbelievably parallel to one another. We must learn to discern how to distinguish between the two. One of the things that really sets the love of God apart is relationship. God's love requires a relationship. In many of the scriptures, Jesus talks about this. He makes statements like, "If I be in you and you in Me…" This is simply saying that we must have an intimate relationship with Him. And we all know in a true relationship there is give and take. Here is the key to God's relationship; it's spiritual and it always seeks to please rather than be pleased. True love seeks to please. We know that the key to lust is that it always wants to take care of *self, first*. Both leave a sense of deep burning down inside as if we are on fire. But what's important is that we *must* determine who the outcome is aimed to please as we stated in the previous sentence. Lust will have you thinking that you are truly in love with someone.

    I found a shocking truth in relationships that I have entertained. Always wanting to be with a person around the clock even when I didn't feel like it was nothing but fear. Love has no fear. As I got older and wiser, I realized that I was afraid of losing that person or being hurt by that person. We had nothing in common and we didn't get along. We were just hanging and feeding our flesh whether it was in sex, recreation or just physical comfort. Know that when you always feel you have to be around or with someone due to fear or being hurt, it is a warning that you need a closer walk with God. Your lack of intimacy with the Lord is causing you to have a lack which is spiritual not carnal. People *cannot* fill that void in you. Stop wasting time and seek God. One of the things I learned is that eventually lust turns to hate. If you do not leave or allow people to leave in the right season, God will allow you to experience pain to wake you up. You feel that you have to be around that person but you cannot get along when you are. Lust will always destroy the relationship. If you want to test a non-marital relationship, try abstinence. Yeah, leave out the sensual part and see how long it lasts?

Man's Worst Enemy

In II Samuel 13:1-18, the story of Amnon and Tamar reveals the truth in this. Amnon, the son of David, had a half-sister named Tamar. The Bible says that he loved her so that he was distressed and became sick. This Hebrew word used for love is "Ahab" - to have an affection for (sexually or otherwise). His affection (desire /lust) to have her was so strong that he began to lose weight. If love makes you sick (for those that are sick for someone)... Hmmmm... After Amnon revealed the secret to his friend and cousin, they conspired for him to sleep with her, yes his own sister (half-sister). In doing so, he forced Tamar to sleep with him. Verse 15 says, "Then Amnon hated her exceedingly so that the hatred that he had was greater than the love he had before." Sound familiar? Now you understand why so many former so-called lovers are greater enemies than they were lovers (kingdom forgiveness can overcome this). It was not love but lust that they entertained.

Reading this passage really shed light on some things in my life. We can easily be fooled by beauty, infatuation and charm. How can you go from loving to hating one day to the next? Not only did he begin to hate her, but he treated her badly. It goes to show when the enemy has gotten what he wants, you are worthless to him... Stop spending your worth for a one-night stand. The moral of the story is this: The two, love and lust, although opposites, are dangerously alike in many ways. Both are spirit therefore working from within, where the spirit brings life, lust brings on death. They are at constant war with one another. This war is for your soul! This isn't a video game; it's real. Every time you get in another sensual relationship you create soul ties that follow you for a life time and affect your future relationships. I feel for those that think they can do anything and make it in. We all are a work in process, but we still have a responsibility. We cannot throw God's grace around.

Fight the good fight of faith and lay hold of eternal salvation. The Holy Spirit of God denies the flesh, which is a must in order to live in Christ (*He that desires to come after me must first deny himself, pick up his cross and follow me*). I believe this is one of the most profound statements given by Jesus. I also believe this is the issue we have with following Him. As we earlier read, in order for us to follow Christ He says that we have to deny ourselves. It is one thing to be denied. But when we are responsible for denying self, this is a totally different dimension. It is one that we too often fail to enter because we cannot live a life of discipline. True disciples are disciplined ones. Many of us are still under the impression that God will allow us to do whatever we please and it's okay. There are some preaching that kind of gospel. Out of love, I beg you to consider your ways. People of God, lust aims to feed the flesh, which is contrary to the will of God. And we know that the carnal mind is an enemy of God because its purpose is to focus on how we feel.

Here is a test for every situation that you are in. When you are trying to discern whether it is of God answer this; does it humble you or does it feel good to you? Does it line up with His word? Please understand, I am one of many past issues and mistakes. I have done others horribly and been done the same. It is out of love that I pen these pages. I love God's people. Thus, I do not aim to blast or condemn. My goal is to reach as many people for Christ as the Lord allows. I learned that love truly covers a multitude of sin. It was in this that I was encouraged and hinge the ministry that God gave me on; when I was acting foolishly and living an undisciplined life, God waited on me! Yaaasssss!!! He waited on me! Therefore, I plan to wait on as many as will hear what I have to say. I don't care where you are in life, there is room at the table for you. As I always say at Epicenter413, "As long as you are breathing, there is opportunity!" There is room at the table. Understand the devices of the enemy and use the strategies that God has left us in His Word. Read it, get it in your spirit, but most of all understand it!

Chapter 6
Deal With the Roots

    Throughout the years of my life as it relates to ministry, problem solving, and things of that nature, I have learned that everything starts some place, especially problems. And what has handicapped the church in many cases is the inability or failure to look beyond the surface of the tree and find the roots or the source of what has developed in people's lives. It is the ignorance of the iceberg characteristics that sank the unsinkable Titanic. There is more to what we see than what we see. There is nothing worse than trying to minister to someone from the wrong angle, which results in them going further away.

    I remember back in the early 1980's when I was about 10 years old. I lived with my mother in an apartment complex in Greenville, SC. I had a friend named Brad who had many issues that I should have run from, but I actually enjoyed being around him (didn't know any better). We used to go bird hunting in the woods near the complex just about every day with pellet guns. Being only 10, he was a full-blown smoker. In other words, he smoked like a grown man. Brad's father condoned his smoking habit and actually bought him cigarettes. I didn't realize the seriousness then, but I began to puff away. It was a daily routine after school, the thing to do. We came home from school, checked in (at least I had to), grabbed our pellet guns and headed into the woods. We found our favorite rock and puffed away. This first began as an adventure, like all bad habits. But what started out as an innocent daily routine transformed into a lifetime of bad habit. That's why it is so important for us to seek God in all of our relationships rather than leaving Him out. Many times, we don't want mom or family to meet and greet in our relationships because we don't want to hear the truth. One major sign that people we meet are not good for us is if we cannot bring them around our loved ones. It's strange how this is the only thing I can remember about this guy is the bad habit I learned from him (something we need to think about). And as I think back, he never stepped foot in my home, but I often spent the night at his house. This was the beginning of a root that would later become a tree that would grow into a Redwood. That Redwood took me nearly 20 years to hew down. But I was going about it the wrong way. Over the years I tried many things to quit but all were futile. I can remember at least 5 times I thought I was clear only to find out later that I was right back into it strong as ever.

When I entered the military in 1989, I was still a heavy smoker at age 18. I smoked all through middle school and high school. I was really looking forward to basic training after finding out that trainees could not smoke. Finally, a force tactic would be the answer to my dilemma, or so I thought! I gave up smoking while in basic training but only because it was strictly enforced. But that's okay, right? At least I quit. Yea, it bothered me for a short while but it was prohibited and I would have had to really go out of the way to get a smoke. Eight weeks later when going through the process for release to AIT (Advanced Individual Training), I remember being at the bus stop waiting for the bus to carry us back to the barracks for our final days in basic training. What did I see except soldiers smoking cigarettes and cigars! Locked away from society with no privileges for nearly three months, I finally had the chance to see the world again. Immediately, that desire returned to me like a ton of bricks sitting on my chest. It was like I saw something for which I had been searching for many years. I tried to restrain myself, but it was too strong for me. Wait a minute. I cut that tree down, right? Needless to say, when I arrived at my next duty station in Georgia, I soon returned to smoking. I was sorely disappointed that I returned to smoking even though I really enjoyed it. It took my breath away, smelt horrible on my clothes, it was a huge turn off, I was embarrassed by it and the list goes on and on. Yet, without much thought I went right back to smoking. Eight whole weeks were down the drain. I had forgotten about cigarette smoking until I got another opportunity. It reminds me of a saying that I once heard about partying; we say we no longer go clubbing. We confess how we have been delivered from those old hang-outs, how we have grown from our former riotous ways. But the truth of the matter is all the clubs and hangouts that we used to hang out at are closed down! It's not that we don't go, we just have nowhere to go anymore. Those old places that we used to go to are no longer available to us. We just don't fit in the new places. Our issue is convenience. But dealing with convenience alone will not solve our issues. It's still in us. Paul says in Romans 11:18 (paraphrased), "The branches do not support the root but the root supports the branches." Unless the root is dried up, the branches will return. What we deal with in most cases is the branches and leaves that we see. However, the problem is in the root. The problem resembles that of an iceberg. What we see is only the tip of the problem. This is the issue we find when dealing with all of our shortcomings. We quickly deal with the branches and when out of sight, it's out of mind. Some roots run deep. And until we dig deep, we will never cause the issues of life to cease.

How did I finally deal with smoking, lust and fornication? I learned by working in my yard. Have you ever watched the flower bed start growing grass one blade at a time? You keep saying, "I gotta get that before it spreads." But day after day you walk by and watch the growth. Finally, when the grass has taken over you put on the gloves and go to work pulling up weeds one string at a time. Then, you realize that you have allowed it to get out of hand. It has taken root and spread. And not to mention the roots run deeply. When pulling them up, they break off. If they break, you have to dig them out and if you fail to pull them out they will return in a matter of time. Now instead of taking ten minutes to clean the bed, it takes hours and much more strenuous work. Our issues are the same.

Look at the story of Saul in I Samuel 15. Saul was given strict instruction by Samuel the prophet to destroy all of Amalek and leave nothing or no one alive. He was even instructed to destroy all the livestock, women and children. God said that He would destroy them because of how they tried to ambush Israel when they came up from Egypt. But when Saul went to the Amalekites, he decided that he would save the king, the best of the livestock and all that he considered good. When approached by Samuel, his excuse was that he did what God said. And furthermore, he did it that he might use it to worship God (my, that sounds familiar). Another excuse was his fear of the people. But here is the problem. God sees what we don't see. God sees the roots beyond the tree. God was trying to destroy a root of bitterness that would follow Israel even until this day!

If you read the book of Esther, you will find that Haman was a descendant of King Agag of the Amalekites whom God instructed Saul to destroy. Yes, God is a generational God. While we look at what is good, God knows what's *best* for our lives and looks at it from a righteous view. What Saul did to please man could have caused an entire nation to be wiped out. But God! This is why it is so important that we deal with the roots and not the tree! Roots represent generations, while the tree represents the present generation. I am so glad that God does not think on our terms. While we make decisions based on what we see, God has laid out this life in the terms of eternity. This is why we pass on generational curses like Saul; we do not kill from the root. We should recognize our issues, spray weed control, then commence to digging up the roots in our spiritual garden. Or else, the weeds will return in another season, stronger than ever. They may seem to lie dormant, but don't get too comfortable. We cut down the tree yet we leave the stump.

Under the right conditions stumps come back to life. I have witnessed this on several occasions. I have cut down many trees in my lifetime. When I failed to deal with the stump, I watched it bud again. Until I had that stump removed or destroyed, I was constantly cutting the branches that revived. We are so relieved that the tree is down that we abort the process of completely destroying the roots of our issues. This is exactly what Saul did and generations later, the Jewish race was jeopardized. We say God wouldn't allow that. Well, that may have been the case here, but it is the principle of God's obedience that we are focusing on. We have children's children in our bosom. My desire is to slay as many generational roadblocks as possible. I want to allow my seed to have the freedom to deal with their own battles, while those that were before me and came through me are minimized. When we leave unfinished business, our children have to deal with it. But if we deal with it, they may not even realize we had an issue. Thus, our issue may not be an issue for them. We leave too much for our children to war with as a result. Do you realize that your babies are going to have to battle what you don't conquer? Our debt, unhealthy relationships, and whatever else we leave unconquered they will inherit. Even if we don't live the life that we feel we are promised, we should at least focus on killing some things so our seed doesn't have to deal with it.

If we are not sure how to get to the root of our issues, take Christ's advice; "Some things come only by fasting and prayer." I found this to be the answer for my nicotine addiction. This smoke thing went on for nearly 20 years until I was twenty-seven years old. It was a spiritual addiction and I needed a spiritual solution. We better count on those deep-rooted issues requiring the deep things of God. Deep calls for the deep is how David laid it out in the book of Psalms. Despite the idea that God is a microwave God, He is the same yesterday, today and tomorrow. There are no quick fixes in God. When we have been wrapped up, tied up and tangled up in spiritual darkness, it takes time and effort partly for the purpose of not returning, teaching us a lesson in the process. Furthermore, we are developing and updating our testimony. So instead of being discouraged, we should thank God for His grace! This battle is not ours; it belongs to the Lord. We just have to show up and watch the fight!

This brings me to another issue that we have in ministry. We have a generation of people thinking that there is no suffering in God. Because we turn our lives over, our suffering is over and we don't have to go through anything. Really? This is the very reason a very high percentage of so-called converts are living in a backslidden state. They have turned away from the gospel. Much worse is this watered-down gospel we are preaching is what got them in this predicament. Instead of teaching the truth about life with God, we relay the hakuna matata message, "No worries, everything is alright." In turn, the converts get frustrated and go back to what made them sick in the first place. We are telling folks to come to Jesus, and God will make everything okay. You will get material blessings and so on. But in reality, we should be alarming converts that we are escaping eternal damnation, a life absent from God that will end in hell!

We serve God for the wrong reason. I serve Him because He saved my behind from a horrible death! I am grateful for eternal salvation! That's why I serve Him! So we must stop dealing with what we see, the tip of the iceberg, which is the portion of the tree above ground. The bigger the tree, the more condensed the roots holding it up. Focus on what you do not see! When I say, it takes fasting and prayer for some things to be dealt with, believe me. Not by might nor by power, but by God's spirit! I get so tired of all the world remedies, listening to what other folk tried, what some wrote in books on how they made the necessary changes, and the list goes on... Like Jacob, it called for a wrestling with God; we went toe to toe! As I began to mature in my walk with Christ, it dawned on me that I was preaching the gospel of freedom, the gospel of good news! Here I am serving a God that parted the Red Sea, held back the Jordan River when it was at its peak season, fed five thousand plus with a can of sardines and crackers, healed a sick woman of 12 years with a touch of His garment, and able to save me to the uttermost!!! But I had no power to stop puffing on cigarettes. Where is the power of God in that?

One day while working at BMW, I had just about enough. I'm too anointed for this mess, I thought. So I said, "Lord, I refuse to eat until you deliver me from these nasty, stinking, expensive cigarettes!" I'm tired of smelling like smoke. I'm tired of hiding to go smoke when I should be free. I'm tired of gasping for breath, coughing and having sinus infections when I have been healed by Your stripes. I'm tired of seeing deacons, elders, preachers and pastors pray like Christ and then go outside and smoke while we listen to the Word in church. But most of all, I'm tired of being a so-called man of God with no power. I had a form of godliness without enough power to quit smoking. But You parted the Red Sea??? Lord, can you deliver Me? The devil is a lie. Desperate times call for desperate measures. If you truly want the things of God, you will seek them.

Our problem is that we have no hunger for Him. God is searching for a hungry soul, not a sorry one. Thirty-six hours later, nothing but water, prayer, and repeating God's promise to give us what we ask (according to His will), I was delivered. But before we shout for victory, I warn you. This was the hardest thing I ever did voluntarily, for my first 27 years of life. It hurt, I was sick and thought I was dying (the old me was dying). I had to leave work early and crawl in the bed two days in a row and cry like a baby. But when I came out, AMEN! Today, twenty years later (2018), it is still a testimony. It was my first real fast initiated because I wanted to get right with God by being a living sacrifice, holy and acceptable to Him. This is why Peter says, "He who has suffered in the flesh has ceased from sin!" My prayer is that whoever is reading this finds their way to a truly victorious life because you learned how to deal with the root and not just the tree. Listen: (In Donald Lawrence's voice) "Giants, they gotta come down; the bigger they are, the harder they fall!" Go get what God has for you. It is for you. The victory is in the root. Face it!

Chapter 7
Don't Ignore Warning Signs

Have you ever been driving and failed to pay attention to the road signs? I know on countless occasions I have been caught up in something other than paying attention to where I was going and find myself in near catastrophic situations. What's worse is that some of these situations, I have been a repeat offender knowing that there was danger ahead if I did not heed the warning signs. Signs are for our safety and they provide vital information. They are not just for display. Every road has warning signs. When we are headed some place, there are always signs to direct us on our way, such as curves, stops, yields, etc. Also, there are danger signs warning us of potential hazards that lie ahead of us. Many of us get lost in the curves and sharp turns in our walk with God because we fail to heed to or understand the signs that God has laid out for us. Yes, God has signs that lead us to a blessed place. The problem occurs when we fail to heed to them as if we have arrived and are not in need of direction. "I got this" is the usual approach that leads to going down the wrong path. A sign is just that, a sign. When we see dark skies, clouds, thunder or lightning, we begin to look for the rain.

Just as there are natural warnings, there are spiritual warnings. Do you really believe God will allow us to enter into a danger zone whereby we will be consumed without warning and protection? Certainly not! There are even times when we don't heed the warnings and God will still divinely protect us. This is called mercy. Even Solomon says that there are signs that are within us that speaks volumes about where we are headed. Hand signals, eye winking, etc. are all warning signs that we are involved in something secretive. I have learned that anytime we are doing things that we cannot share with those around us, we are more than likely not pleasing God. Look at the following passage in the message Bible:

"Riffraff and rascals talk out of both sides of their mouths. They wink at each other, they shuffle their feet, they cross their fingers behind their backs. Their perverse minds are always cooking up something nasty, always stirring up trouble. Catastrophe is just around the corner for them, a total smashup, their lives ruined beyond repair." Proverbs 6:12-15 (MSG)

Wow. I bet that will step on some toes. I know because it stepped on my toes, feet and ankles. If you think about what Solomon is saying, these are warning signs that there are major issues on the horizon preparing a storm that will wreak havoc. Until recently, I never thought of it in that manner. When I used to wink, nod my head, make the private jesters, God was trying to tell me something. "Catastrophe is around the corner." Don't ignore these signs; hiding your wedding ring, winking, second looks, etc. These are signs that you are preparing to engage in some foolishness.

The importance of being in tune with God is discernment. Relationship is so important, but it is most lacking. I heard a former associate make a statement like this about church folk; "We are in last place, among the most lacking, always the sickest, in the worst shape but we are the most churched!" First of all, this is a serious indictment against the church. Here is a man that has left the church for what I feel was some type of hurt, as I stated earlier, thinking service to Christ makes life short of tribulation. However, his statement was so profound and full of truth. I don't deny truth. People please hear this; we as 'the church' culture are the most churched, yet we are the least progressed. This is serious. Why? Because we refuse to deal with those secret sins and fail to be disciplined. That simply means that we are churchin' and not changn,' we have revelation without manifestation! It ought not be so. We are all responsible for our own, but woe unto him who offends the weak-minded causing them to lose hope. The principle cause of this is lack of personal relationship with God. We are so quick to flock to gifts, talents, callings, status, material things and the likings, that we fail to see God. This was Isaiah's issue until God removed King Uzziah from his vision. Then, he saw that the Lord was the true KING. We call ourselves blessed and highly favored since we have acquired a certain possession or position or favor with a certain man or woman. Do we realize what being "blessed" means? And if we are so blessed, it is solidified with relationship. A true blessed vessel is characterized by the blessing that he is to others. We are blessed to be a blessing. Possession does not equate to blessing. It just becomes the fruit thereof. When we go secure a loan for that new car, house, etc. it is not necessarily due to our being blessed. God's blessing "makes one rich and adds no sorrow" (Proverbs 10:22). Last I checked, payments don't make us rich! But this misconception of 'anything is alright with God' is just a manifestation that most church going folk are not in tune with the spirit of God.

I am making these statements by experience and knowledge. I have the knowledge because the Bible teaches me that most people do not have a relationship with the Father, yet they talk the most. I have experience because I haven't always been where I am. And being a pastor is neither here nor there for me. In other words, I don't claim to be experienced because I am a pastor, but because I have lived and learned many things through my mistakes and watching others make mistakes. It is a choice. God says if we draw nigh unto Him, He will draw nigh unto us. There is no discernment without relationship with the Holy Spirit. A majority of church discernment is "street smart," which simply means what you see reminds you of what you have been through! It means that you are in tune with it because you once dealt with it. Or you watched NCIS. But you are calling it discernment.

As I often remind the members of Epicenter413 where I serve as pastor, our attitude reflects our level of relationship with Him. Our attitude determines our altitude. I'm sorry but you been saved how long? And you still haven't been delivered? Talking about "that's just how I am." Oh, God can't change your attitude? You will not convince me of your relationship with Him without first showing me your fruit of the Spirit. Then, at that point we can discuss your level of discernment. Why is this so important? Because He has to dwell with you and that is only possible in a sanctified vessel. He knows the mind and will of God for us and towards us. How can we live without Him? How can we survive without Him? This is the heritage of the saints. He is the one who leads and guides us into all truth. He is the one who warns us of danger. So many things happen to us because we refuse to listen to the warning system that God strategically placed inside us! When things happen in our lives we think, "Where did that come from?" as if it happened overnight. Negative. This thing has been building in us for a while. We just failed to listen. We have been building and nurturing this for many years. It was a slow fade, eating away at our integrity, killing our testimony, dulling our anointing! This is why a relationship is so vital. I'm not talking about a relationship with the world but with the Creator! While we were winking, sighing and making hand motions, it was building a bridge. At the same time, if you had been in tune with God's warning signs, it would have prepared you for the danger ahead. I am convinced of the benefits of a faith relationship with God. It equips us with the ability to see things we may not completely understand, but we trust enough to avoid the catastrophic ending that Solomon referred to.

    Sometimes I just look back at times that I didn't understand why it didn't work out; the relationship, the deal, the job, etc. and I realize it was God making divine interventions in my life so I could detour a rough road or even an ending one. Often I find myself on the other side of the valley wondering how I made it over. I have to take a praise break right there. My God, when I look back over my life and see some of the seen and unseen dangers He spared me from, my soul cries out "HALLELUJAH!!!" Don't ever forget what God has done. Not saying that I got it all right, but I'm saying that God has a plan for my life and He wants to detour me of the roads that will lead me to destruction. Sometimes I did not heed. But His grace and mercy said, "OH NO, we've already paid the price!" I would much rather heed the warnings that I may please Him even more.

With that being said, pay attention to your eyes, hands and words. Learn your secretness and know that God is warning you of what lies ahead. Stop saying, "I got this" or "I didn't mean anything by it." Remember what the writer said, your secretness is "cooking up something nasty, always stirring up trouble" and "catastrophe is just around the corner." Your big issue began as a small thought. Take authority over your life! This is not a game. It's war. He (the devil) is after blood. He wants your life in exchange for death. While you are playing and enjoying the fun, know that it is temporary and the cost is more than you are willing to pay in the end. Ask Moses. Hebrews 11:24 says, "By faith Moses, when he became of age, refused to be called the son of Pharaoh's daughter (25), choosing rather to suffer affliction with the people of God than to enjoy the passing pleasures of sin…" Are you willing to give up your place in this 'passing' world to suffer the same afflictions as the people of God? Maybe we just need to 'come of age' like Moses and 'come to our senses' like the prodigal son! Moses did not fear the king, but regarded God and the riches in Christ greater than this current world. Whatever it takes, whatever the case, get there. Find the Moses in your situation and make it happen. With what Christ has done in and for us, we no longer have an excuse. If He did it for Moses, He can and will do it for you. We have absolutely NO EXCUSES! And guess what? Moses ain't got nothing on you! He looked *to* the reward while you look *from* the reward! Praise Jesus!

Chapter 8
Embrace Your Suffering!

Now here is a subject we all would love to avoid. In fact, I believe that this next subject is one of the main reasons many Christians fail to get to the level of deliverance and freedom that they are called to. Yes, we are entitled to a level of deliverance and freedom that allows us to live in victory instead of revisiting that same old issue day in and out. The level of victory we should desire is called *rest* and this is what Jesus meant when He said, "Come unto Me all that are burdened and heavy laden and I will give you rest..." Most believers are "burdened and heavy laden" and the fullness of God is not yet manifest. Why, because we are still in bondage to something other than the spirit of the Lord? Oh, we may no longer go to the clubs and such, but why? Is it because we are delivered or is it because those clubs that we went to are no longer in existence? Is it because we cannot do the dances? Or is it because we are embarrassed to be seen knowing we have so-called transformed our lives? Whatever our answer tends to be, we are only truly delivered and free when all the opportunities exist and we choose not to participate rather than not having opportunity. Absence does not equal deliverance or freedom. I know you would like it if God Himself removed all of your problems, addictions, bad habits, evil desires, and shortcomings as soon as you became saved. In fact, I think it would be safe to say that most of us pray and / or expect this, which eventually leads to a disappointment that causes a falling away. What I mean is that when we have unrealistic, non-scriptural expectations of God as a result of false or surface-level teaching and understanding, we find ourselves being disappointed and we tend to lose faith in God. Do your homework. God is not some fairytale that will deliver you at the shaking of a stick. Face it! Who has said, "I want to suffer for God just like Jesus did?" No one has other than Paul that I am aware of! So, allow me to let you down as easy as possible; it will not happen! We have to realize and preach this fact: Christianity is no fairytale religion unlike many immature believers as well as religions portray it to be. In fact, we live a lie knowing we are not living the life of victory but rather a defeated, continual cycle of past hurts and experiences. Bandages, drunkenness, lying, hiding and other temporary solutions keep us living an endless cycle that worsens as it turns. That is why Jesus says in John 8:32, "You shall know the truth and the truth shall make you free," and again in verse 36, "Whom the Son has made free shall be free indeed." Nothing but His Word has the power to free you from any addiction that the enemy has brought about to destroy you and *it will free you*. This age old, not new, love of pleasure has one antidote; His name is Jesus. So many of us are waiting on God to come like Calgon and take us away. Worst off, preachers are preaching that our breakthrough is coming regardless of how we live. This actually grieves my spirit to hear this being taught without teaching God's people that there is a righteous requirement from us. It is called repentance. Here is the newsflash: you need to break free from sin before God brings a breakthrough. Jesus was manifest to destroy the works of the devil! God is not a fairytale that will take our problems away and bring us into a place where we are no longer faced with those things again. Sorry to bother your religion, but I speak from experience of having had to come face-to-face with each and every one of the major issues in my life that have ever hindered me.

There comes a point in your life that you must go toe-to-toe with yourself and your issues as Jacob did, knowing that God will never put more on you than you can bear. If there is no enemy within, then the enemy outside can do us no harm. That is the real enemy. But without a fight, there is no victory. How can you have victory without struggle? We can apply this to every aspect of our lives... But even in this we have to understand God's Word. We (including me) are quick to say, "The battle belongs to the Lord." This is so true. But please understand that this does not excuse us from showing up at the battle site. Let's put this in perspective; God fights the battle while we keep the faith. In other words, the battle does belong to Him but Paul tells us in Timothy that we have to fight the good fight of faith. God is not moved by crying and sorrow. Without faith, it is impossible to please Him. Where is your faith?

On top of all of this, the Bible reminds us that even though we think this is about us, the battle really has nothing to do with us. It belongs to God. Now that's something to shout about because every situation we encounter, we have what it takes to handle it according to II Peter 1:3 which says, "As His divine power has given unto us all things pertaining to life and godliness..." What it means is that we are anointed for it. If He brought us to it, He has seen us through it. Somebody needs to know that every situation encountered is a victory in Him. Know that it may not seem good, but it is definitely working for our good. Yes, someone may have meant an act against us for evil, but God has turned it around for our good if we love Him. So in our future experiences, we shouldn't panic. We must ask God to show us that divine power that works in us so that we may be able to get victory in every situation.

Now, on to the point that I am trying make, let us read I Peter 4:1 which states, "For as much then as Christ has suffered for us in the flesh, arm yourselves likewise with the same mind: for he that has suffered in the flesh has ceased from sin!" Let me say it this way, if you will; there comes a point in life that you must suffer through some things. Yes, I said it and I know that most don't want to hear that and may lose interest in reading right here. But I speak truth to power. This is God's way of killing your flesh. Last time I heard, dying was not an easy task but rather difficult. Hear what the Spirit says; sin is defeated through suffering (I Peter 4:1). Glory to God, this is how Jesus defeated death, hell and the grave, through suffering. He submitted Himself to God and denied the pleasures of life to bring us to an eternal glory much greater than what we see.

Let me explain something to you. My wife and I were divorced for three years. During this time, I began to draw nigh unto God and God began to draw nigh to me as a result of my desire (you have to be hungry!). I was hurt as if my heart were ripped out of my chest. At this point in my life, I was so dysfunctional that I had no clue who I was and had no reason to live. It was during the twenty-five to twenty-seven-year range of my life and I was full of failures, fears, and wicked desire having made not some but all of the wrong decisions based on my desires. I was a mess. Yet through all of this I felt the call of God on my life. I knew only one thing: I needed a drastic change. I had no one to turn to so I could share my REAL issues. I was a loner and felt like no one wanted to hear my issues, nor was I bold enough to confess my internal struggles. It was all a cover up, a deep well of hurt, pain, suffering (the kind that kills), no direction, laden with sin, buried in lust and a whole lot of fear. Actually, it was strange that I saw people in my corner but they really didn't know who I was or where I came from. I was an expert, masked man. I felt so fake not because I wanted to but because I thought I was the most dysfunctional human being on the planet and others thought I had it all together. Yes, I shared some of my story but only the surface. No person had ever personally entered my heart to see my pain to truly minister to me. When they did approach my heart I ran and no one cared enough to pursue. This would be the way I entered the pulpit, saved but not delivered and in a world of hurt, shame and confusion. I wasn't ready but I was pushed because of the gift.

    Don't let anyone push you before you are ready. Yes, I still had major issues when I accepted the calling on my life. This is the indictment that I have against the church. We promote the gifts but ignore the character. Instead of getting to know men and testing their faith, we promote based on the assets brought to the table (i.e. finances and charisma). As I began this journey, I became more aware of what I was dealing with. The driving force in my life was clear to me; the spirit of lust and shame kept me on the run. These things pushed me but in the wrong direction. The thing that really threw me was that as I began to enter below the surface of my life through His Word, it kept getting stronger and stronger. I thought, now as I get closer to the Lord, surely this desire would fade away. Instead, it became a reality. This thing was so powerful that I almost lost it! Thank God for the blood! So yes, I denied myself in many cases trying to please God and walk upright before Him by walking away from fornication and other selfish motives. I let go of some relationships that were not of God in order to flee temptation.

    The point I am trying to make is that I thought it would eventually leave me, but it just seemed to get stronger and eventually I fell into a trap relationship headed straight to hell with a one-way ticket. I was in a relationship, preaching God's Word and fornicating at the same time. The feeling of lust was so strong that it became overwhelming! I felt as if I were getting married again because of lust. But God intervened and changed the wind.

    You can't tell me that He doesn't hear a sinner's prayer. I could tell you a thing or two here. However, within a year my wife and I were remarried and trying to work things out (God's plan). I just know that sometimes He does the impossible because He can. The first few months were pretty good considering the past. However, over the few years we were divorced, I realized something that was rather disturbing. Outside the suit and tie, being saved, and a few years older, I was the same ole boy. This is when it really hit me and I knew if I didn't do something quickly I was going to die. Yes, I felt like God was going to literally kill me. I don't understand how some of the most influential people in ministry are not convicted or at least seem that way. I learned that the more powerful my ministering becomes, the more God requires of me. I feel as He releases His anointing to me, I need to release my life to Him in the form of obedience and character. I tried fasting, denying, praying, fleeing and many other tactics. But as time went on and believe me, even though I was not engaged with anyone other my wife, it was clear that I still had a serious problem. It was as if she could not satisfy me enough and I was still lacking something. This was not about her and what she was doing but about what was happening in me. On top of this, my wife began to go through some major challenges which led to her having to focus on her life. This affected her physically and mentally, ending up in major surgery. It seemed as if all was spiraling down except that old desire that drove me. Then came the real trial. How can I keep myself while she was dealing with her pain and suffering?

    At this critical point in my life God, allowed my wife to go through some deep issues and her focus was definitely not on pleasing me, in fact far from it. This is when I realized what the Lord was trying to do in me. Though at first and for a long time I thought, "God hates me and has set me up to have an embarrassing run and He wants to make an example of me." After some time, not a short time, I am talking years of suffering, I began to look at the man in the mirror. Then, I began to understand that He was not only working something in me but He was working something in her, too. It was a hard pill to swallow. But this is the epitome of selfishness, expecting our spouse to save us when they are fighting the same life battle that we are fighting, working out their own salvation. This is when I had to face it. I fed this beast so long that he had completely consumed my life, my thoughts. But what really hurt was the fact that everyone thought I had it all together. It was if everyone looked past my struggles. I finally did the unthinkable; I began to take inventory of my life, my spirit and even my soul. At this point I really began to seek Him for real deliverance, something that a church could not do.

In my studies, I learned that suffering is inevitable if you are going to consider yourself a son of the king. This is a thing that I must suffer through in order to get through. This was not a revival service breakthrough. I couldn't pay my way through it. No one would be able to lay hands on me to get me out of it. Lust was there from my childhood to destroy me and had led me to this point. It attracted folks to me on an assignment to destroy me. I once remember going to a conference in Easley, SC where Tommy Bates, Pastor of Community Family Church of Independence, Kentucky, was the speaker. I was still battling trying to figure this thing out, about to go crazy in a stand-still battle for my life yet the church could not see it. I figured, either I was a good cover up, or they were blinded by their own issues, or they just didn't care. Where is the discerning spirit of the church? Anyway, while at the conference, he

(Tommy) had the place on fire. I was on the very front row. He was going around laying hands on others and they were falling out all over the place. Finally, he headed in my direction. I'm not sure if I wanted it but he stepped to me and said, "You already got it!" He did not lay hands on me but looked me right in my eye and said, "You already got it!" This was a pivotal point in my life. I then realized that God was trying to tell me all along that He was my source and the power was within. Reality set in; I had to suffer through this one! Then, I understood what it was Jacob wrestled with the angel about, himself. Every man must come to the point in life where they must meet God face-to-face. I had to come to reality with myself and say to God, "I refuse to come here to this place in my life and allow you to leave without change. I don't want to let you go." Many of us are on the verge of change, real breakthrough (not this dolla and holla stuff being preached). However, we let go before the breaking of day. This wrestle would be the wrestle that eventually freed me from the stronghold that led me those 30 some odd years. I almost let go, feeling death on my back.

I really don't understand how some claim to be sons of God and actively engage in sin consensually and unending. I understand the season of struggle, believe me I do. And I would never condemn because God waited on me. Something is wrong with that picture but that is not my glory. I just know I couldn't continue life being bound by anything other than that which saved my soul. I had to suffer through for a long time in the form of not being satisfied and glorying in the Lord at the same time. You do know that satisfied flesh is always sorry. We ought to get tired of saying sorry and forgive us for the same things day in and day out. Finally, I realized that any and everything that hinders us and causes us to go astray was defeated on Calvary. I just chose to bring it to life by not dying to it. I am convinced that freedom is a decision, as life is a series of choices. I am free because I choose to be free. The rest is history and God's story. When you decide to allow God to fight your battle and you fight the good fight of faith, victory belongs to you.

    I can remember back many years ago how it all began. At first when I recognized I had a problem that I could not deny, it didn't matter as much because I fulfilled my desire and fed it. However, when the Lord saved me and I grew closer to Him, inevitably it was no longer acceptable. The only thing that changed was going from being open to incognito even from myself. I pretended as if I were delivered from it. I walked around faking it, hoping I was making it. I looked like the ideal brother living the life with nice cars, clothes, home, etc. I was "living the best life," so they thought. I tried everything under the moon, including church. But when I tried Jesus, Amen! Some things have to take their course. It's like a cold; you can take all types of medicine but at the end of the day you have to suffer through it. "Arm yourselves likewise. For he who has suffered in the flesh has ceased from sin!" (1 Peter 4:1)

Chapter 9
God's Word Will Keep You

Throughout our walk with the Father, there are many benefits that come with the relationship. We are so misinformed because we don't seek the Lord with all of our heart. Being so concerned about 'getting blessed,' we fail to go through the process by listening to false, prosperity messages.

My people are destroyed for the lack of knowledge. Because you have rejected knowledge I will reject you from being priests before Me. Because you have forgotten the law of your God, I also will forget your children.
Hosea 4:6

Hosea tells Israel about their lack in the knowledge and help of the Lord. Because we fail to go to the Father for His guidance in our lives, we are rejected from our position. Position is important to us all, especially, but not limited to, when men are not in their place as kings, priests and prophets. There is much to say about this, but we will not get into it at this time. Thanks to God for those praying women that have filled the gap. I cannot fathom where we would be without them. But here Israel is told by God, "Because you have rejected my knowledge, I will reject you from being my priest." *AND* "I will forget your children (paraphrased)." This is vital to our lives that we serve God in the position as priests before Him. We must function according to our purpose, lest we lose hope.

Man's Worst Enemy

Solomon says it best in Ecclesiastes 10:7, "I have seen servants on horses while princes walk on the ground like servants!" This is not right people of God. And we are mad at those in all types of position as if it is their fault we (God's church) are walking like servants. Learn to take responsibility for where you are in your life and stop the blame game. I see this so much in the marketplace. People are supposed to be serving but they are in high places (they are in high position but out of place) and God's people living like their servants. We whom God has given authority are angry with them. We are out of place just like they are! We are where we are because we are not ready! We must get into our position so that we receive our inheritance. This should lead us to seek God for providence and direction in our lives. If we want to get angry, we must get angry with ourselves! Some of us reading these words right now know that we are out of position and headed for destruction because of a lack of vision in our lives. How can we see over the mountain called life when we are always in the valley? This leads me to the reasoning behind this chapter. Now let us put knowledge into play pertaining to the number one enemy in regards to failure in men's lives, the crafty harlot. There is hope and there is help. Listen to what Solomon advises:

"My son keep your father's command, And do not forsake the law of your mother. Bind them continually upon your heart; Tie them around your neck. When you roam they will lead you, when you sleep they will keep you; when you awake they will speak with you. For the commandment is a lamp and the law is a light; Reproofs and instruction are

the way of life, to keep you from the evil woman, from the flattering tongue of a seductress. Do not lust after her beauty in your heart, nor let her allure you with her eyelids. For by means of a harlot a man is reduced to a crust of bread; and an adulteress will prey upon his precious life. Prov 6:20-26 (NKJV)

God's Word will keep you from the powerful lure of lust. If you think this is just pertaining to women, you're wrong. This pertains to every aspect of our lives where lust or strong desire and covetousness is trying to take the focus from the love of God, whom it is forever trying to imitate. Solomon says in verse 23, "His commandments are a lamp and His law is a light to keep us from the evil woman." We don't have to wonder how so many men cannot escape the snare of women; how that the greatest of kings, the best of men, the anointed of the Lord, and all walks of people are destroyed by the craftiness of lust because we do not know nor do we take heed to the law of the Lord which keeps us. Verse 22 tells us that even when we roam it (the law, commandments) will lead us. The Lord knows that we are like sheep gone astray. But a sheep with the law and commandments of the Lord on his heart will be led even in times of roaming (to roam is to walk at ease), when we are more likely to roam out of God's perfect will in our lives. Many times, because of who we think we are, (strong enough to escape at the right time, "I got this" type of attitude) we feel safe when we are in danger. Note that lust is referred to as a snare, a trap, or crafty, etc... He (desire) doesn't come at you dressed up with a sign on his forehead saying, "I am your enemy and

I have come to kill you, steal from you and destroy your life." While we think we are okay and in control, we linger and play these silly games with lust but listen to what Solomon says to us;

"Can a man take fire in his bosom and his clothes not be burned? Can one walk on hot coals and his feet not be seared?" Prov 6:27-28 (NKJV)

Please understand; when we play with fire, we will be burned. This is serious business that God is not tolerating from His people. Judgement begins with us, in God's house. He called us out of the darkness that we should walk in the light. When we walk in the light we know that we are His! In Numbers 11:34 after the people complained saying, "Give us meat…" God waited until they received what they complained about and lusted after (strongly desired, coveted) and killed them calling the place "Graves of Craving." God was angry that the people couldn't transition out of Egypt because desire was so strong that they were "weeping throughout their families everyone at the door of their tent," crying, "give us meat to eat." Imagine that, walking down the street of your neighborhood and folks crying and lamenting, "We want meat to eat. We are tired of what we have." Moses was so frustrated and I can understand why. This thing is deeper than a woman or a man. It is a spirit.

How do we maintain in times of want? We rely on God's Word. Peter tells us that everything we need pertaining to life and godliness is found in the knowledge of Christ (2 Peter 1:3). This is not about trying to be super spiritual. This is as practical as it gets. We don't need another tactic. The plans are laid out for us. The blueprints are complete. We need the truth of God's Word. We have too many distractions that we are presenting to men and women trying to appeal or satisfy their outward symptoms when all we need is this Word. We do any and everything to appease but when did His Word stop working? This is the reason I didn't want to write a book, become a pastor, etc. We have too much of that. Books are a dime a dozen (probably less now), and pastors are too easy to come by and too hard to trust. This is not about five steps to your breakthrough, name it and claim it, etc. This is simply the Word of God unto salvation and I am no longer ashamed of it. It has the power to raise us up out of mess and give us a message. It has the power to break every chain of who we used to be. It has the power to loose the stronghold and destroy the yoke so we can be what God created us to be. But it also has the power to expose us if we continue in sin. We don't need anyone to lay hands on us. We don't need anyone to pray for us. All that is good in its season, but what we need is to repent and speak the Word of God over own lives and some people to hold us accountable. Stay away from those that don't confront you about the life you are living and get around some folk that love you to life.

Know and seek to understand Solomon's wisdom. Look at this passage concerning God's wisdom in Ecclesiastes 7: 25-26:

I applied mine heart to know, and to search, and to seek out wisdom, and the reason [of things], and to know the wickedness of folly, even of foolishness [and] madness: And I find more bitter than death the woman, whose heart [is] snares and nets, [and] her hands [as] bands: whoso pleaseth God shall escape from her; but the sinner shall be taken by her.

Notice that he first applied his heart. Application is the key to God's Word. Be a doer and not just a hearer. So he applied his heart to know, search, and understand. This is when revelation comes, when we truly seek God in our hearts and apply it to our lives. Now here is the wisdom God reveals to him: Solomon says that more bitter than death is a woman whose heart is set on entangling and snares. In other words, it is better to die than to be entangled in the snares of a woman. Of all the things that Solomon sought and learned, being the wisest on earth, he warned viciously about the woman and her bitterness. Listen to Solomon's experience; He has come to realize more than ever the evil of that great sin which he himself had been guilty of, the *loving of many strange women,* (1 Kings 11:1). In fact, these were the women that he was warned not to mingle with. He is now lamenting as a result of his failure to follow instruction. He found the recalling of this sinful way of life very grievous and heavy upon his conscience. Oh, the agony that he encountered even at the thought of it—the wickedness, the foolishness, the madness, that he had been guilty of, *"more bitter than death."* The mere reflection of it terrorized him, as if he had been under the arrest of death. This conviction cries out against him; they are bitter as gall, **nay**, bitter as death, to all true penitents. Listen to Solomon, the temptation to this sin is very dangerous, and it is extremely difficult, *next to impossible*, for us to venture into this temptation and escape the sin. Furthermore, those that have fallen by it stand little to no chance of repentance. The heart of the adulterous woman is a heart of *snares and nets;* her game is played with intent to ruin souls with as much deceit and subtlety as any fowler used to take a silly, roaming bird. The unwary souls are tempted into these snares and nets by the bait of pleasure, which they greedily catch being promised of satisfaction. However, they are taken before they are aware, and taken irrecoverably.

    My goodness, this is so obvious in today's society. Lust gets strength through gratification and its charms are more prevalent. But listen to what he says of God's favor to any man if by his grace he has kept him from this sin: *"He that pleases God shall escape from her."* Either he will be preserved from being tempted or from being overcome by the temptation. Those that are kept from this sin must acknowledge it is God who keeps them, and not any strength or resolution of their own. As for the women who read this, it should serve as a warning to you to avoid being used by satan. In addition, please understand how the enemy desires to use you as a tool to destroy men of God. This is why it is important for us to be God pleasers that we may escape the snare. It took some time but I learned the complexity of this subject, how that it was a dream killer, a soul snatcher and a king assassin. You want to destroy an anointing? Here you go. And for all the ladies out there, men also are in this category whom Paul mentioned in 2 Timothy 3:5, 6 who "Having the form of godliness, but denying the power thereof; from such turn away." Verse 6 says "For of this sort are they which creep into houses, and lead captive silly women laden with sins, led away with diverse lust..." Lord have I seen my mothers, daughters and sisters led away because they are trusting men who seem to be anointed by God but have not the power of God. Ladies, married and single women, guard your heart with all diligence and stop falling for potential and look at the reality. No man should privately come to you in any situation, especially as a married man and one in leadership. That is out of order and it is a set up! Let's get this thing right!

Chapter 10
Pursue, Overtake, and Recover All

On November 12, 2006 as I was reading God's Word, the Lord spoke to my heart. While reading this particular passage about David's prelude to becoming king, I began to think back on some things that I have gone through and the life that I forfeited in Christ to pursue me and who I thought I wanted to be. So many times, I risked my life in pursuit of things that felt good but did not satisfy my soul. There are years I wasted, relationships I destroyed, children I let down and the list goes on. On this night in 2006, as I read the book of I Samuel concerning David's life before the kingdom reign, I found in I Samuel 30:6 that David comes to a point where he is greatly troubled and distressed. While absent from his house, the enemy comes in and steals all that he has and burns the remains that were left, taking all his wives, children and possessions. Instead of focusing on the issues that they ALL had, the men that were with David blamed him and even spoke of stoning him. What do you do when after you have helped folk change their lives and given them hope, they turn on you because of what the enemy has done? Not you, but the enemy? The Bible says that David "encouraged himself in the Lord." If no one is there to encourage you, you must encourage yourself. David has come to a place in his life where he knows that people will not always be with him in life's struggles, even those that are closest. We have to find a way to encourage ourselves in the Lord and love them, too! Now here is the catapult of this message; after the Ziklag experience, David goes to the Lord and inquires about how to handle this situation. Many of us just accept loss and try to move on. Pick up the pieces and let it go... But the fact of the matter is we have suffered a great loss. Our dignity is gone. Our joy is gone. Even our love as well as all the other things that are attached to it are gone. I am not sure about you, but I suffered a great loss. I was in pain with a belly full of regret. My feet had slipped, not *almost slipped but slipped*! When I finally realized my loss, it dawned on me that I could not recover. A quick fix would not solve this issue. In fact, I was tired of Band-Aids. I didn't need another temporary breakthrough. I was tired of patches in my spiritual life. I needed a completely new beginning.

Many times, we have auto accidents and the vehicle may be damaged, but we cannot see the extent of the damage. It looks good on the outside but the insurance company totals the car. The damage is internal; the frame is bent. This is an image of my life. I looked good from the outside, but I was bent on the inside (full of iniquity): broken and torn beyond human repair. I was so confused and bound by so many habits I was using one habit to cope with another. Here is David, damaged goods. He lost everything that was dear to him. Instead of just moving forward, he inquires of the Lord, "What shall I do? Shall I continue on Lord? Shall I go after my dream, my hope, my joy, my inheritance?" I like that he was willing to accept ONLY what God confirmed. The Lord answered him and said, "Pursue, for thou shall surely overtake them, and without fail recover all!"

Three Commands God Gives to David

▷ <u>Pursue</u>- The enemy destroyed David and his men's homes and took their spoil. The Lord told David to pursue (run after with hostile intent, chase, put to flight, hunt, persecute) his enemy. Once you recognize what your enemy has taken and are in agreement with God, pursue. The kingdom of God suffers violence but the violent take it by force. We cannot sit by idle while the enemy robs us of our dreams and blessing that God gave us. Just make sure what you lost was yours. Many of us are chasing things that do not belong to us.

▷ <u>Overtake</u>- The Lord told David to overtake (to attain, take hold of). God has given us permission to go and get what the enemy stole from us. We not only have a "dunamis" anointing (miraculous power of God) but we have "exousia" or authority to overtake the enemy. The dunamis (miraculous power of God) is for the excellence of soul. It is what we have from God through Christ to heal the sin sick soul and to live right and destroy the yokes that the enemy placed on us through sin. When we are saved, we are saved through this dunamis. But we also have to activate the exousia (authority) anointing in order to live free. It is the authority to walk in complete victory. Many of us are walking in blessing but we don't have total victory over our lives; no freedom. Exousia is the authority over the devils that haunt us daily when we don't have the authority to drive them away. It is the anointing that the Seven Sons of Sceva lacked when the demon said in Acts 19, "Jesus I know, and Paul I know; but who are you?" We all know how that story ended, butt-naked, afraid and haunted by demons that they tried to cast out!

When we are born again we cannot be possessed but we can surely be tormented when we don't have exousia or authority to overtake our territory! I pray that God grants you understanding and gives you authority over your life. Without exousia, we will never take control of our lives. This is the "power and authority" that Jesus gave the disciples in Luke 9:1.

▹ <u>Recover all</u>- God says to us; everything that the devil stole, we can get it back. Just make sure what you lost was yours. As stated earlier, we often want to pursue what we lost and it was never ours. It was not the best for our life. This is why we should always seek God and *choose our battles.* Don't fight every fight you encounter. It may not be meant for you to recover some things in some cases. Losing some things in my life was the best thing that happened to me. I am very relational and I love people but some people had to go. I was cleaning out my closet one day and ran across some new clothes that I never wore. My closet was full but I could hear God saying, "Give it away. You have too much in your life to receive." Learn to make room for God to bless you. He will not bless a storehouse but He is looking for a warehouse. Understand the difference in "loss" and "making room." Let that one soak in. Somebody lost some stuff and they are pursuing it only to miss out on what God is really trying to do in their life. *Remember; the blessing of the Lord makes rich and adds no sorrow...* Ask God!

Chapter 11
That 'BEST' Life

My question to you today, not tomorrow, but today is this: what kind of life do you want to live? Many people will say that they are living that best life. When in reality they are living a good life (in some cases a not so good life). They have most of the things they desire. They are comfortable where they are career-wise. They are just experiencing some good things at this point in life. Calling borrowing blessing... Again, you do know that the blessing of the Lord makes you rich and adds no sorrow; God's blessing adds no payments, no worries, etc.? Before I sought to understand what blessing REALLY is, that was me. I would always say that God is good, His favor is upon me, I am living the life. Yet deep inside God was saying, "Son, come up hither." I was holding down one of the best jobs in the Upstate, making six plus digits. Most of my bills were paid. I finally got that bachelor's degree in management that I always wanted. My family was taking vacations. I was tithing and giving. I had some struggles but I was doing some things that a man of God would like to do and then some, or so I thought. THEN, God finally won the battle of many years with regards to my wife and I stepping out in ministry (I fought it tooth and nail for years). I finally yielded and said, "Okay Lord, this is it, you win." We did the Steve Harvey jump (so we thought). Lady Lee and I posted on social media that we finally jumped (in the voice of Steve Harvey). We have finally stepped into that life of faith that God has called us to. We stepped out of the ministry that we were in and returned back to the man and woman of God that taught us true ministry (I would like to add that this was a major decision and very humbling).

At first it was great, humbling, and seemed noble all at the same time. But the struggle of humbling ourselves was real (at least for me). Fifteen months later Epicenter413 was birthed. Now we are sailing on supernatural faith. Are we? Well, let me tell you that God allowed me to think that for just a moment. We quickly came off that high horse when I heard Him saying, "Are you truly trusting Me with your life?" Well, I thought we were Lord. I mean we are doing the unthinkable, (for me at least), in ministry. We dared do this being that we are young, have no following, stepping out on the front line! Are we living by faith? Are we Lord?

Now let's take a deeper look at this. We don't take it lightly, the ministry. But let me inform you of something. Ministry is your purpose in life. It is all of our purpose to be attached to ministry. Our purpose is to glorify God and to win souls for Christ. God has equipped us with gifts to walk in that we are to use to bring others to the kingdom. This is purpose. The thing I learned about purpose is that God is responsible. We are responsible for bringing the faith to the table. He created us for it. He will perform it until we go home… But them dreams though, a different arena. Let me tell you saints, when you begin to walk in the purpose that God ordained for your life, it will open the doors of your dreams. Yasssss! Purpose opens the doors to your dreams. This is a different type of faith. Everyone does not have the faith to walk in dreams. It takes a supernatural gift of faith. So, when we begin to walk in purpose God says, "Now those dreams you were having..." My God, my God. But hold up a minute. This dream is big. It is scary. What if I fail? What if it is too much? Listen to me people of God; if your dream is too small, it's not God. If it is attainable through you, then it is not the "big one" (in Fred Sanford's voice) that God gave you. If your dream seems bigger than you, it's because it is much bigger than you. However, I felt a different level of faith was needed to walk in a dream world versus walking in ministry.

    See, with Epicenter413, I am learning the Moses technique. Moses led the people but not without God. He was quick to remind God that Israel did not belong to him. I'm talking to pastors, ministry leaders and anyone leading God's people in any capacity; trust God to provide direction and provision. Stop trying to take God's place. I remember being in a meeting with a group of prominent pastors when one of them was having trouble resting. When asked why, he stated that he could not sleep due to always trying to figure out the next move of God. He only slept two or three hours nightly. Wow. I advised him to give God back that ministry and stop trying to be Him. Needless to say, I left the group. I can't be God. I'm taking vacations and I'm learning the gift of "no." I have (still a bit of a struggle) the gift of goodbye. I learned that God is the only one who can deal with folk's heart. I just try my best to love unconditionally and stay away from church cliques! I'm going with the Word and not the biggest giver, the most knowledgeable, most influential... you catch my drift?

What it boils down to is this; in order to get that best life, you have to be willing to release that good life. I know it is secure. I know you like it. I know you are comfortable. I know that it promises a descent ending. But all of that I just mentioned is the problem. A true life of faith is unattainable by our means and it will not come to pass waiting on retirement. It will not manifest in mediocrity. It will not show up while you are comfortable. It will not come to pass waiting until you get that letter of retirement. All of those are dream killers, hired to frustrate your purpose in life. Your best life is waiting for you on the other side of faith. Habakkuk 2:4b says, "The just shall live by his faith." Show me a man or woman living by faith and I will show you someone who has sacrificed all those things that we mentioned, including their greatest fear. You HAVE to 'bust a faith move' if you intend to please God. Most of us are playing it safe, waiting on a blessing to fall out of the sky, waiting to hit the lottery (yes that too), that big break, retirement! Let me slow down. I don't want to spoil the fun. If you want to dive into that best life, purchase my second book, *Get Busy Living OR Get Busy Dying,* coming late 2019. It is based on leaving the life of mediocre to a life of faith. It's not about 'stuff' but about the power and freedom of God being released in your life. It is about walking away from and breaking the cycles that keep us coming to a complete circle in our faith which causes us to eventually become ineffective in life and ministry. It's about seeking God (not chasing Him) and seeing the stuff, even the desires chasing us. It's not a prosperity message but a message of what real prosperity is. Oh yeah, I thought I was living the life. But trust me, about 95% (my hypothesis) of God's people think the same way yet are living in fear or chasing stuff. The most active but the least trusting. Get the book!

Chapter 12
Deal With Your Beast!

I can remember one morning being sleepless as I got out of my bed and began to pray. As I prayed, I began to meditate on some people that I came in contact with over my life and how they are living to this day. I could not help but wonder what type of role I played in their lives. I know that every man must face God for himself. I cannot help but wonder if I caused anyone pain that led to failure. This is a hard pill to swallow. Thus, I repented for the life that I lived, regardless of how I got this way. There was this beast within me seeking whom it may devour. I never meant to harm anyone, but I had no control over my mind or body.

As I look back, I can understand why I would love and leave. It was the beast within me that would not allow me to love. We cannot go back and change what we've done, who we've hurt. We can only change what we are doing. I do believe that we should pray for the healing of those that we are responsible for hurting. It is so obvious in people's lives that they have been hurt by others whom they loved or trusted. When we allow him to use us to do such, we then are responsible for the hurt we've caused. I won't talk of the faces of those who I have caused hurt. This is not so hard when you know that God has anointed us to come back from our hurt no matter how devastating. But I want to bring it home. Look at your face. Can anyone see the beast in you, especially those reading this book who KNOW they have not been delivered from within? As for me, I looked like a gentleman in all aspects. However, within I was driven by everything but God. This is what is so scary about people and trusting them. You can't put anything past anyone. This is why the church is being exposed because there are a lot of hurting people who need healing and a lot of people that need deliverance.

Why come to Jehovah Rapha and fail to receive healing? Is there no balm in Gilead? Is there no Physician there? Get your healing. Get your deliverance. Or go home and stop hiding behind the church. All have sinned and fallen short of God's glory. So, do what you have to do to get what you need. Work out your own salvation. I learned to turn that beast of desire over to God. He is the only one who can handle your giant but you are the only one who can show up at the fight and claim the victory. Jesus says that it is better to enter into eternal life maimed or missing a limb than to be whole and enter into eternal damnation (Mark 9:43 paraphrased). Deal with your issues. That's why we came to God because we did not like who we were. We came because we could not handle it. If you are going to go to God's house, you may as well go ahead and claim your prize, the high call of God in Christ. I am like Jacob; I refused to and I continue to refuse to leave this place until He blesses me in my mind, in my body and in my soul. Get your healing. Get your freedom. Stop chasing stuff and seek God. I'd rather be free and in good standing with my Father than to be a beast inside and the richest man on earth. Stop making your family hurt. They know you are struggling with this thing. But they cannot do it for you. Neither can that man or woman of God that you are more loyal to than your family.

God bless and I pray that He gives you grace to finish strong.

Note to Readers:

I pray that this reading has blessed your life. Please don't take it personal. In order to experience healing there must first be a revealing. My desire is to see men and women who struggle with lust and addictions delivered that they may be used by God. So many of us kingdom folk are tied up and tangled up in the chains of desire. I find many as my wife's uncle Charlie used to say, "you making a lot of noise" but not saying nothing! We have a desire to serve, but we are tangled in the affairs of this life. The alternative to total submission to God is continued sexual, inappropriate sin in our homes, communities and churches. One thing is for sure concerning God's people: He is fed up and we are being exposed. We serve a mighty God, who is not slack in His promises. But what we count as slackness is actually His mercy patiently waiting on us to line up with His will. If you are in battle with the trials of life, submit to God and the enemy will flee. Let the rest of your life be the best of your life! Those of you that are truly living by faith, I bid you God speed. As the writer in Hebrews 11:2 says, "By faith you obtain a good report or testimony" (paraphrased). Stay strong in the Lord and the power of His might. He will reward the faithful at heart. Our goal is to help our brothers and sisters in need. There is a Balm in Gilead!

Need help?
Please contact us via
https://www.reggiestoddardministries.com/

For publishing opportunities, contact
HadassahsCrown@gmail.com

www.ingramcontent.com/pod-product-compliance
Lightning Source LLC
Chambersburg PA
CBHW050437010526
44118CB00013B/1566